OCCASIONAL
P A P E R

# Revisiting US-VISIT

## U.S. Immigration Processes, Concerns, and Consequences

David S. Ortiz, Shari Lawrence Pfleeger,

Aruna Balakrishnan, Merril Miceli

 INFRASTRUCTURE, SAFETY, AND ENVIRONMENT

The research described in this report results from the RAND Corporation's continuing program of self-initiated research. Support for such research is provided, in part, by donors and by the independent research development provisions of RAND's contracts for the operation of its U.S. Department of Defense federally funded research and development centers. This research was conducted within RAND Infrastructure, Safety, and Environment (ISE), a unit of the RAND Corporation.

**Library of Congress Cataloging-in-Publication Data**

Revisiting US-VISIT : U.S. immigration processes, concerns, and consequences / David S. Ortiz ... [et al.].
    p. cm. — (Occassional paper ; OP-140)
    Includes bibliographical references.
    ISBN 0-8330-3912-1 (pbk. : alk. paper)
    1. United States—Emigration and immigration—Government policy. 2. France—Emigration and immigration—Government policy. 3. Visas—Government policy—United States. 4. Visas—Government policy—France. 5. Terrorism—United States—Prevention. 6. Terrorism—France—Prevention.  I. Ortiz, David (David Santana) II. Series: Occasional paper (Rand Corporation) ; OP-140.

JV6483.R472 2006
325.73—dc22

                                                                                        2006001872

The RAND Corporation is a nonprofit research organization providing objective analysis and effective solutions that address the challenges facing the public and private sectors around the world. RAND's publications do not necessarily reflect the opinions of its research clients and sponsors.

**RAND**® is a registered trademark.

Published 2006 by the RAND Corporation
1776 Main Street, P.O. Box 2138, Santa Monica, CA 90407-2138
1200 South Hayes Street, Arlington, VA 22202-5050
4570 Fifth Avenue, Suite 600, Pittsburgh, PA 15213-2612
RAND URL: http://www.rand.org/
To order RAND documents or to obtain additional information, contact
Distribution Services: Telephone: (310) 451-7002;
Fax: (310) 451-6915; Email: order@rand.org

# Preface

The United States Visitor and Immigrant Status Indicator Technology (US-VISIT) program incorporates new technology, processes, and changes to immigration law across multiple federal departments and agencies. Although a system for recording the arrival and departure of nonimmigrant visitors was mandated by Congress in 1996 through the Illegal Immigration Reform and Immigrant Responsibility Act (IIRIRA), concerns about congestion at border crossings delayed its implementation. A specific program to address the mandate was not designed until it was spurred by the terrorist attacks of September 11, 2001, in New York, Pennsylvania, and Washington, D.C. The technological aspects of US-VISIT include biometric visas, passports, scanning equipment, linked databases, and the recording of the arrival and departure of nonimmigrant aliens. Federal agencies involved include the U.S. Department of State (DOS), which issues visas and passports and negotiates international standards for biometric identifiers, and the U.S. Department of Homeland Security (DHS), including U.S. Customs and Border Protection (CBP) and U.S. Citizenship and Immigration Services (USCIS). The US-VISIT information systems link several databases, including a watch list of known immigration violators and other criminals, a system for storing information on foreign students, and a database of previous visa holders. The system became operational at all ports of entry at the end of 2005 with the goal of covering all nonimmigrant alien visitors to the United States. Since the program incorporates biometric technology, relies on systems that must be widely accessible, and cannot impede travel and trade involving visitors to the country, the system's design and implementation raise many issues regarding personal privacy, technology, and security.

This paper discusses some of the policy issues raised by the introduction and development of US-VISIT in an effort to inform discussion and support good decisionmaking. To assist the understanding of the technology, privacy, and security implications of the system, we present a case study of France's visa requirements implemented in the late 1980s and early 1990s, measures taken in direct response to terrorist bombings in the 1980s; France's actions then are similar to many U.S. actions now, and lessons can be learned from the consequences.

The paper is current as of March 2006. The issues discussed should be of interest to members of Congress, policy analysts and organizations concerned with personal privacy and information technology, and those interested in the effects of immigration policy on national security.

This occasional paper results from the RAND Corporation's continuing program of self-initiated research. Support for such research is provided, in part, by donors and by the independent research and development provisions of RAND's contracts for the operation of its U.S. Department of Defense federally funded research and development centers.

## RAND Infrastructure, Safety, and Environment

This research was conducted within RAND Infrastructure, Safety, and Environment (ISE). The mission of RAND Infrastructure, Safety, and Environment is to improve the development, operation, use, and protection of society's essential physical assets and natural resources and to enhance the related social assets of safety and security of individuals in transit and in their workplaces and communities. The ISE research portfolio encompasses research and analysis on a broad range of policy areas including homeland security, criminal justice, public safety, occupational safety, the environment, energy, natural resources, climate, agriculture, economic development, transportation, information and telecommunications technologies, space exploration, and other aspects of science and technology policy.

Questions or comments about this report should be sent to the project leader, David Ortiz (David_Ortiz@rand.org). Information about RAND Infrastructure, Safety, and Environment is available online (http://www.rand.org/ise). Inquiries about ISE projects should be sent to the following address:

Debra Knopman, Vice President and Director
RAND Infrastructure, Safety, and Environment
1200 South Hayes Street
Arlington, VA 22202-5050
703-413-1100, x5667
Debra_Knopman@rand.org

# Contents

# Figures

# Tables

# Summary

In January 2004, the U.S. Department of Homeland Security (DHS) inaugurated a new system for the tracking of foreign visitors at ports of entry to the United States: the United States Visitor and Immigrant Status Indicator Technology (US-VISIT) program. The rollout occurred at 115 air and 14 sea ports of entry. Visitors with nonimmigrant visas found that to gain entry to the United States, they needed to submit to a photograph and a fingerprint scan. DHS claims that the photograph and fingerprint add only a few seconds to the inspection time for each visitor but give DHS the opportunity to verify identity and to compare the applicant against text-based and biometric watch lists maintained by law enforcement agencies. Furthermore, the U.S. Department of State's new visa procedures require all visitors needing a visa to apply in person for the travel document, at which time a digital photograph and fingerprints are collected and incorporated into the US-VISIT system. The US-VISIT requirements were extended to visitors from the 27 Visa Waiver Program (VWP) countries in October 2004. To remain eligible to enter the United States under the VWP, travelers from these countries must possess a passport containing a digital photograph if that passport was issued after October 26, 2005. The system has also been implemented at the 50 busiest land ports of entry. Exit kiosks are being installed at ports so that visitors can record their exit from the United States.

Fundamentally, US-VISIT is an electronic system for verifying a traveler's identity and ensuring that the traveler is not sought by a law enforcement agency. Congress mandated that the U.S. Immigration and Naturalization Service develop a system for monitoring visitor access to the United States in 1996. Congress subsequently deferred the program's implementation from October 15, 1998, to March 30, 2001, fearing increased congestion at U.S. border crossings (U.S. Department of Homeland Security, 2005). However, the attacks of September 11, 2001, provided a motivation for development and implementation. Now, DHS entities U.S. Customs and Border Protection (CBP), U.S. Citizenship and Immigration Services (USCIS), and U.S. Immigration and Customs Enforcement (ICE) maintain and operate the US-VISIT system. The US-VISIT system consists of user terminals, databases, and communication links that allow a CBP inspector to collect a visitor's biographic and biometric information and compare it against criminal watch lists, lists of foreign students, and accepted and rejected visa holders. US-VISIT is being implemented in four increments, with the first initiated in January 2004, and the final configuration of the system available near the end of the decade. Proper operation requires the coordination of the component databases, each of which is monitored by a different government agency, and the maintenance of the communication links among the subsystems. Because US-VISIT data are personal and sensitive, care is required to maintain personal privacy and security.

In the mid-1980s, when France was the victim of a series of terrorist attacks, it tightened its immigration and visitor controls by means of the "Pasqua Laws." Visa requirements were imposed on all visitors from countries other than those of the then–European Community, and Liechtenstein, Monaco, Andorra, and Switzerland. The European Community convened meetings on appropriate responses to terrorism, including increased airport security. Affected nations, including the United States, reacted negatively to the new requirements, processes, and procedures for obtaining a visa. Within France, there were complaints of program mismanagement and warnings of deleterious effects on travel and trade. There are many parallels between France's actions in 1986 and U.S. actions today in response to terrorist attacks. Imposition of a visa requirement in France seems to have had no long-term negative economic impact on trade and tourism; the visa requirement led to an initial drop in immigration that persisted for several years. The international community seems to have understood that a trade-off can be made between free access and national security. Similar drops may be less desirable in the United States, particularly for seasonal workers and students. The effects of the French visa requirements were felt in the context of a larger, intentionally restrictive immigration policy; US-VISIT's effects must be viewed in the same larger context, with reasoned consideration of what the United States would like to accomplish through regulation of immigration and border controls.

These lessons, coupled with a detailed view of the workings of US-VISIT, enable us to identify key policy questions that should be discussed as the system is implemented, and expanded throughout the decade. These questions include the following:

- How can database and communication links be made reliable and available?
- How can the user interface be designed to speed processing and minimize human error?
- How can the design of US-VISIT ensure privacy and incorporate fair information practices, including limitations on the government's ability to collect and disclose data inappropriately, guarantees of security, and opportunities for stakeholders—including the foreign visitors themselves—to petition for redress and correction of the data?
- How can US-VISIT guarantee proper coordination among the disparate government agencies that control data used by US-VISIT to segregate legitimate travelers (such as students, tourists, and business visitors) from criminals?
- How can US-VISIT and related processes, such as Department of State consular services, be monitored so that the United States can minimize their effects on legitimate travel, trade, and tourism?

These policy issues in particular, and our analysis in general, suggest several targets of future inquiry.

1.  US-VISIT is a complicated technological and interagency-implemented system that will affect all visitors to the United States. An independent analysis of US-VISIT com-

ponents and processes from a systems engineering standpoint would help to set standards for system operation and maintenance to ensure seamless coordination among databases and systems.

2.  US-VISIT collects personal information from foreign travelers. Many countries, in particular those of the European Union, have far more stringent regulations regarding the collection and use of personal data. An analysis of the extent to which US-VISIT complies with these laws would aid the United States in promoting the system abroad. Additionally, cultural considerations regarding the collection of photographs and fingerprints should be addressed.

3.  US-VISIT monitors only legal visitors to the United States. It is imperative that DHS quantify the costs and benefits of US-VISIT in the broader context of overall border control.

4.  Proponents and critics of US-VISIT should be patient in evaluating the system. A lesson from France's immigration policy changes is that the initial shock of the policies had short-term effects, but tourism and trade recovered over time.

# Abbreviations

| | |
|---|---|
| ADIS | Arrival/Departure Information System |
| APIS | Advance Passenger Information System |
| CBP | U.S. Customs and Border Protection |
| CCD | Consular Consolidated Database |
| CIPRIS | Coordinated Interagency Partnership Regulating International Students |
| CLAIMS | Computer-Linked Application Information Management System |
| DHS | U.S. Department of Homeland Security |
| DMIA | Data Management Improvement Act |
| DOS | U.S. Department of State |
| FBI | Federal Bureau of Investigation |
| FMEA | Failure Modes and Effects Analysis |
| GAO | Government Accountability Office |
| HSPD | Homeland Security Presidential Directive |
| IBIS | Interagency Border Inspection System |
| ICAO | International Civil Aviation Organization |
| ICE | U.S. Immigration and Customs Enforcement |
| IDENT | Automated Biometric Identification System |
| IIRIRA | Illegal Immigration Reform and Immigrant Responsibility Act |
| INS | U.S. Immigration and Naturalization Service |
| IT | information technology |
| MOU | memorandum of understanding |
| NCIC | National Crime Information Center |
| NSEERS | National Security Entry-Exit Registration System |
| OECD | Organization for Economic Cooperation and Development |
| OMB | Office of Management and Budget |
| OSTP | Office of Science and Technology Policy |
| OTM | "other than Mexican" |

| | |
|---|---|
| PNR | Passenger Name Record |
| POE | port of entry |
| SEVIS | Student and Exchange Visitor Information System |
| TIPOFF | U.S. State Department Terrorist Database |
| TSC | Terrorist Screening Center |
| TTIC | Terrorist Threat Integration Center |
| USCIS | U.S. Citizenship and Immigration Services |
| US-VISIT | United States Visitor and Immigrant Status Indicator Technology |
| VWP | Visa Waiver Program |
| VWPPA | Visa Waiver Permanent Program Act |

# CHAPTER ONE

# Introduction and Motivation

U.S. border control is a daunting task. There are hundreds of official ports of entry, including 216 airports, 143 seaports, and 115 land crossings (Wasem et al., 2004). U.S. borders are long and difficult to patrol. The land border with Canada stretches 5,525 miles and contains only 84 land ports of entry; the Mexican border is 1,933 miles long with 25 land ports of entry. The 143 sea ports of entry service 12,479 miles of coastline. Over 800,000 people enter daily into the United States from Mexico alone. These border crossings support the U.S., Canadian, and Mexican economies (Wasem et al., 2004). Improper management of border crossings can have a significant effect on trade, tourism, and international cooperation.

Modernization of the U.S. border crossing system was mandated in 1996 in section 110 of the Illegal Immigration Reform and Immigrant Responsibility Act (IIRIRA; P.L. 104-208). The law required all ports of entry to the United States to collect and maintain electronic records of all foreign arrivals and departures.[1] Congress subsequently deferred the program's implementation from October 15, 1998, to March 30, 2001, fearing increased congestion at U.S. border crossings (U.S. Department of Homeland Security, 2005).[2]

However, the attacks on the United States on September 11, 2001, changed the U.S. government's and society's perspectives on border protection. Both the USA PATRIOT Act of 2001 and the Enhanced Border Security and Visa Entry Reform Act of 2002 responded to the fact that some of the September 11 hijackers had exploited holes or violated their status in the U.S. visa and immigration system. For example, the single hijacker who had entered the United States on a legal student visa failed to arrive at his stated academic institution. Most others entered legally on tourist visas, though it was determined later that many had falsified information on their visa applications or overstayed the terms of their visas. Famously, immigration officials approved a change in status to Mohammed Atta's visa in September 2002, two years after he applied for the change and a year after the attacks. Better record keeping at the border would surely improve public safety, it was reasoned, especially when coupled with

---

[1]    Data to be collected include name, address in the United States, biometric identifiers, visa status, flight identifiers, and additional information based on visa type (such as a student's location of study and names of family members).

[2]    For example, the press noted that there was "fear that that the implementation of this law may cause U.S. ports of entry to become severely congested" (Latour and Lleras, P.A., 2000).

actions by the U.S. Department of State, law enforcement, and educational institutions. The IIRIRA recognized the deficiencies in the border-crossing record keeping system and mandated changes well before September 2001.

In January 2004, the U.S. Department of Homeland Security (DHS) instituted the United States Visitor and Immigrant Status Indicator Technology (US-VISIT) program to fulfill the directives of the IIRIRA and other related legislation. Initially, the system operated at 114 U.S. airports and 15 seaports. It expanded to include the 50 busiest land ports of entry on December 31, 2004. Systems for collecting data regarding foreign visitors exiting the United States will be designed and implemented while obstacles—such as the unavailability of airport space—are considered and addressed. The goals of the US-VISIT program are to

- enhance the security of citizens and visitors,
- facilitate legitimate travel and trade,
- ensure the integrity of the immigration system, and
- safeguard the personal privacy of visitors.[3]

The IIRIRA also mandated the development of additional systems, all of which have been incorporated in the US-VISIT program. For example, the IIRIRA required that an electronic system be developed to collect foreign student information from colleges and universities. Subsequently, a pilot program, the Coordinated Interagency Partnership Regulating International Students (CIPRIS), was developed and tested from June 1997 to October 1999. Beginning in July 2001, the U.S. Immigration and Naturalization Service (INS) developed a new system to replace it, the Student and Exchange Visitor Information System (SEVIS). Colleges and universities opposed both systems because they were cumbersome to use and because a fee, currently $100, was levied on foreign students (U.S. Immigration and Customs Enforcement, 2004). Nevertheless, the USA PATRIOT Act of 2001 mandated the full implementation of SEVIS by January 1, 2003, and also required the implementation of the US-VISIT program. The Enhanced Border Security and Visa Entry Reform Act of 2001 added requirements to the US-VISIT program regarding its interoperability with law enforcement agencies.

The challenges for US-VISIT and other visa issuing and processing systems are significant. In 2004, the United States hosted 46.1 million international visitors, representing a 12-percent increase from 2003. The U.S. borders with Canada and Mexico are particularly busy. For example, the Canadian border handles $1.4 billion in trade each day, but "most of Canada's 160 land and maritime border crossings have only one person at the posts" ("Report: Canada's Border Not Secure," 2004). Similarly, "the U.S.-Mexico border is the busiest worldwide. Over one million people cross the border every day. Over 193,181,314 people crossed the border legally during the fiscal year 2002" (U.S. Embassy in Mexico, undated). Unfortunately, too many illegal aliens slip through the border. "Mexico accounted for nearly 69 percent of the total unauthorized resident population in January 2000,"[4] and Passel (2003) estimates that

---

[3]  See U.S. Department of Homeland Security, "US-VISIT: How It Works" (undated).

[4]  U.S. Citizenship and Immigration Services (2003a).

430,000 illegal entrants cross the Mexican border each year. Bowers (2005) points out that a large number of illegal Mexican immigrants to the United States "are automatically turned back at the borders," while citizens of other countries "are allowed in, pending immigration hearings. These others are referred to as 'other than Mexicans,' or OTMs, by the Department of Homeland Security. . . . They come from other Latin American countries as well as other parts of the world, many of them designated by the government as countries of 'special interest.' In 2004, some 44,000 OTMs were allowed into the [United States]."

The US-VISIT system must process each legitimate foreign traveler's entry and exit from the country, validating travel documents and checking the petitioner against criminal and terrorist watch lists. Visa categories can be complex. For example, "the Immigration and Nationality Act provides two nonimmigrant visa categories for persons wishing to study in the United States. The 'F' visa is reserved for nonimmigrants wishing to pursue academic studies and/or language training programs, and the 'M' visa is reserved for nonimmigrants wishing to pursue nonacademic or vocational studies" (U.S. Citizenship and Immigration Services, 2005c). An H-1B visa is given to a nonimmigrant alien who will be employed temporarily in a specialty occupation or "as a fashion model of distinguished merit and ability." A holder of an H-1B visa must be sponsored by an employer and, with certain exceptions, can remain in the United States for up to six years (U.S. Citizenship and Immigration Services, 2003b). The rules and regulations for each visa type are complex, and the complete system of border controls must reconcile all relevant laws and add to the safety of the population and its visitors while encouraging legitimate travel, trade, and education.

The analysis contained in this report is motivated by the interactions of US-VISIT with the U.S. government's other immigration, law enforcement, and educational information systems and goals. Any foreign visitor to the United States must submit to processing via the US-VISIT system. Viewed in isolation, US-VISIT is not a particularly interesting program: It collects biographical and biometric information from travelers and maintains records of travel. Its usefulness and possible pitfalls derive from coordination with other information systems, designed for different purposes. For example, universities must participate in SEVIS if they are to enroll foreign students. These foreign students procure visas through the U.S. Department of State. The US-VISIT system accesses both the visa database and the SEVIS system to determine if a student should enter the country. It is in the coordination of these systems where the true policy issues surrounding US-VISIT exist. This paper investigates the structure of the US-VISIT system as well as the motivation for its implementation at this time.

Proponents of US-VISIT highlight its ability to provide the United States with more effective border control, addressing the need not only to keep terrorists out but also to deal with illegal immigration and trade. Critics decry the invasion of privacy, the unwelcoming message that it sends to visitors, and the possible resulting decline of trade and tourism. We address each of these issues, separating what is known from what is surmised. To assist us in understanding the likely effects of US-VISIT, we investigate the experience of France in the 1980s, when the first "Pasqua Laws," implemented to stop terrorism and illegal immigration, required visas from visitors who previously had needed none. We conclude by framing the issues that should be addressed by the United States as US-VISIT continues to be implemented, expanded, and improved.

## Analysis Goal and Methodology

This paper presents a framework for evaluating the effects of US-VISIT on U.S. national security, international cooperation, and legitimate travel and trade. Our aim is not to determine whether US-VISIT is a good or bad program but rather to assist government, citizens, and interested parties in understanding and assessing its impact on affected people and organizations.

### Analysis Goal

The goal of this analysis is to identify key policy issues concerning US-VISIT, putting them in context with respect to international precedents and the costs and benefits of welcoming non-immigrant visitors to the United States. To realize this goal, we view US-VISIT as a dynamic system for controlling U.S. ports of entry, not as a static set of policies and procedures. Indeed, the system continues to be implemented and expanded. We assess its benefits and risks in the context of its use. For example, since the sites for the US-VISIT pilot program are publicly known, we examine whether it is possible to evade the safeguards of the system simply by altering travel plans. Anecdotal evidence suggests that travelers are changing planes outside the United States to avoid obtaining transit visas from the U.S. government; we look at the implications of such avoidance for trade and tourism. We also examine the degree to which the mandates of US-VISIT are realistic. For instance, the United States requires travelers from Visa Waiver Program (VWP) countries to obtain passports containing verifiable biometric identifiers, but not all countries are on target to meet that mandate. We investigate whether delays to the system, coupled with concerns about privacy and data protection, hamper legitimate trade and sour international participation. We seek to assist DHS as it creates and assesses development strategies that allow for effective, efficient system rollout and testing with enthusiastic international support.

### Research Methodology

We have drawn our methodology from previous RAND Corporation analysis. US-VISIT is a program to enhance enforcement of U.S. immigration law through the application of information technology and regulatory processes. RAND has studied such systems in the past, and to achieve our goals here, we adopt an approach similar to that of Anderson et al. (2003). That study, commissioned by the State of California, assessed the utility of the California Department of Information Technology as it was about to be disbanded.[5] To determine what could be learned from other states with exemplary practices in information technology (IT) governance, Anderson et al. conducted case studies in Virginia, New York, Pennsylvania, and Illinois. The research identified a number of common factors (most of which did not at that time characterize California's approach to IT governance) likely to account for successful information technology programs, including:

- Executive leaders who are champions of IT and who emphasize its value for achieving state missions

---

[5]   The disbanding of the department was due to a sunset clause in its enabling legislation.

- A management style that is participative and collaborative, that emphasizes "carrots" over "sticks," and that evidences a commitment to employees during periods of change
- A modular and incremental approach to development and implementation of IT initiatives.

Based on the lessons learned in the case studies, the researchers made recommendations for a new agency of information technology in California and described a set of challenges that such an agency is likely to face.

In a similar manner, for this study we performed a series of tasks designed to elucidate the fundamental issues regarding the implementation of US-VISIT and then used a case study to highlight lessons learned from a similar program implemented in France; the results of the French experience may be useful as US-VISIT is implemented.

At its core, US-VISIT is a data collection, analysis, and verification system. It collects biographical data, fingerprints, and photographs from visa-bearing nonimmigrants, and from those travelers entitled to enter the United States under the VWP, and compares them with the same traits collected by overseas consulates, U.S. academic institutions, and law enforcement agencies. Our research methodology addresses the effect of the collection and comparison on the parties involved: the travelers, various DHS entities, the U.S. Department of State (DOS), the transportation media (airlines, drivers, railways, ships, etc.), and the recipients of goods and services provided by the travelers. Our approach has four steps:

1. Describe the context for the implementation of US-VISIT and discuss its technological structure, processes, and deployment plan.
2. Review the literature, including reports in the press and government assessments, and generate quantitative evidence of US-VISIT's effects on travel, trade, and security.
3. Evaluate the actual effects of a similar program in France, the Pasqua Laws, enacted in 1986 in response to a series of terrorist bombings in Paris, to determine lessons that can be learned and applied in the United States. In particular, we investigate whether the dire predictions about the Pasqua Laws (predictions that are similar to current-day predictions about US-VISIT) matched the reality of implementation.

Using the results of steps 1 through 3, we identify the issues surrounding US-VISIT, and suggest a framework to be used for discussion and analysis among stakeholders in the system.

# CHAPTER TWO

# US-VISIT Context and System Description

## Legal Mandate

Responsibility for visas and border control is shared by DOS and DHS, as outlined in a memorandum of understanding (MOU) signed on September 28, 2003 (*Memorandum of Understanding*, 2003). The MOU, authorized by Secretary of State Colin Powell and Secretary of Homeland Security Thomas Ridge, defines the relationship between the departments and implements section 428 of the Homeland Security Act of 2002.[1]

There are key differences in agency responsibility. DHS has the following responsibilities:

- Establishing U.S. visa policy and reviewing its implementation
- Approving all immigrant and nonimmigrant petitions for visas and naturalization documents
- Granting permission to work in the United States
- Issuing extensions of stay, and changing or adjusting an applicant's status while the applicant is in the United States
- Assigning staff to consular posts overseas to provide advice to consular officers regarding security threats that concern the adjudication of visa applications. DHS staff may also review visa applications and conduct investigations involving visa matters.

The DOS is responsible for

- Leading and managing the consular corps
- Managing the visa process and executing U.S. foreign policy
- Visa adjudication and issuance, through its Bureau of Consular Affairs, although its recommendations are subject to DHS consultation and final approval[2]

---

[1] Section 428 of the Homeland Security Act of 2002 addresses visa issuance and makes explicit which activities are in the purview of which Department. "The State Department will continue to manage the visa process and the foreign policy of the United States. DHS will establish and review visa policy, and ensure that homeland security requirements are fully reflected in the visa process" (U.S. Department of Homeland Security, 2003a).

[2] Complete information about the U.S. Department of State, Bureau of Consular Affairs is available on its Web site, http://www.travel.state.gov (as of January 6, 2006).

- Determining visa validity periods, but DHS is consulted before DOS establishes or increases any period of validity.

Several Homeland Security Presidential Directives (HSPDs) regarding terrorist screening and agency coordination are relevant to US-VISIT. HSPD 2 addresses "Combating Terrorism Through Immigration Policies" and was issued on October 29, 2001. It mandated that a Foreign Terrorist Tracking Task Force be created by the Attorney General no later than November 1, 2001, with the following goals:

> (1) deny entry into the United States of aliens associated with, suspected of being engaged in, or supporting terrorist activity; and (2) locate, detain, prosecute, or deport any such aliens already present in the United States. (Bush, 2001)

The Attorney General, the Secretary of Treasury, and the CIA Director were instructed to advise the INS and Customs Services on how to improve investigative and intelligence analysis.

Because of loopholes in the foreign student visa process that enabled terrorists to participate in the 1993 and 2001 World Trade Center incidents, the Secretary of State, the Attorney General, the Secretary of Education, the Office of Science and Technology Policy (OSTP) Director, the Secretary of Defense, and the Secretary of Energy were instructed to work with academic institutions to create tighter controls for issuing student visas in an effort to hinder the training of foreign nationals in ways that could harm the United States. The directive also asked the OSTP and the Office of Management and Budget (OMB) to provide assistance with technology and budget concerns, respectively.

To ensure that trade and legitimate travel continued unhindered between the United States and both Mexico and Canada, the Secretary of State, Secretary of the Treasury, and the Attorney General were instructed to work directly with appropriate Mexican and Canadian authorities to increase immigration and customs information-sharing and, potentially, to develop a common control data base with both countries.

HSPD 6 addressed the "Integration and Use of Screening Information" (Bush, 2003). The Attorney General was directed to establish a central organization responsible for screening for terrorists and collecting and using information about terrorists. Originally called the Terrorist Threat Integration Center (TTIC) and now called the Terrorist Screening Center (TSC), this organization receives all terrorist information from executive departments and agencies. The Attorney General determines at which opportunities screening will be conducted.

The Secretary of Homeland Security develops guidelines for using this information in state, local, territorial, tribal, and private screening processes. HSPD 6 directed the Secretary of State to propose a plan for cooperating with foreign governments to gain access to their terrorist screening information.

Building on HSPD 6 and the creation of the TSC to implement a "coordinated and comprehensive approach to terrorist-related screening" (Bush, 2003), on August 27, 2004, HSPD 11 addressed "Comprehensive Terrorist-Related Screening Procedures" (Bush, 2004). The Secretary of Homeland Security was directed to submit 75 days later a report that outlined a strategy for improving terrorist screening. This report was also to describe opportunities for screening, protocols to be used, and more. It was to be followed in 15 days by one that described an investment and implementation plan, including "the scope, governance, principles, outcomes, milestones, training objectives, metrics, costs, and schedule of activities" (Bush, 2004). The meaning of "terrorist-related screening" in this directive was very broad: "the collection, analysis, dissemination, and use of information related to people, cargo, conveyances, and other entities and objects that pose a threat to homeland security. Terrorist-related screening also includes risk assessment, inspection, and credentialing" (Bush, 2004). The directives provide the context in which US-VISIT must operate, and each affects the design and implementation of the system.

There are several laws relevant to US-VISIT. For example, the Immigration and Naturalization Service Data Management Improvement Act (DMIA) of 2000 requires development and deployment of an entry and exit system to record the arrival and departure of every visitor to the United States (Immigration and Naturalization Service Data Management Improvement Act, 2000).[3] Previous U.S. entry procedures required a passport, visa (if appropriate), and a statement of travel plans and contact information. US-VISIT augments these procedures with biometric identifiers that can be verified at the port of entry (and, in the future, at the port of exit). The DMIA prohibits immigration authorities from imposing on any visitors to the country new entry or exit documentation requirements for the purpose of collecting data for US-VISIT. The DMIA created a task force to examine border and entry traffic and electronic data systems for immigration checks. This task force comprises 17 officials from six federal agencies, two state and local governmental groups, and nine private-industry trade and travel organizations. After September 11, 2001, the USA PATRIOT Act urged the swift development of the entry and exit program and also recommended reviewing the use of biometric identifiers to establish "a technology standard that would be used in the development of the US VISIT System" (U.S. Department of Homeland Security, 2003c, p. 2). The Enhanced Border Security and Visa Entry Reform Act of 2001 and 2002 furthered this interest in biometrics by increasing "requirements for US-VISIT System integration, interoperability with other law enforcement and intelligence systems, biometrics, and accessibility."[4] The rules affecting citizens of Canada, Mexico, and countries participating in the VWP vary according to the visitor's intent.[5] Under the initial law and regulations, Canadians are not required to

---

3   An automated alien entry/exit system is mandated in five laws. The original intent of the reform was to track aliens and to ensure their departure at the termination of their visas. The focus of laws since September 11, 2001, has been to increase border security. The applicable laws are the Illegal Immigration Reform and Immigrant Responsibility Act of 1996 (IIRIRA; P.L. 104-208), the INS Data Management Improvement Act (DMIA; P.L. 106-215); the Visa Waiver Permanent Program Act (VWPPA; P.L. 106-396); the Uniting and Strengthening America by Providing Appropriate Tools Required to Intercept and Obstruct Terrorism Act (USA PATRIOT Act; P.L. 107-56); and the Enhanced Border Security and Visa Entry Reform Act (Border Security Act; P.L. 107-173).

4   This information is available from U.S. Department of Homeland Security, "Fact Sheet: US-VISIT Program," (undated).

5   The Visa Waiver Program (VWP), initially implemented in 1989, allows citizens holding passports from certain designated "visa waiver" countries to enter the United States without a visa. Authority for the VWP is contained in section 217 of the Immigration and Nationality Act (8 U.S.C. 1104[a]) and was supplemented by the Visa Waiver Permanent Program

have visas upon entering the United States as tourists, and the requirement for them to present passports is to go into effect at all border crossings on December 31, 2007.[6] Similarly, foreign national tourists entering the United States pursuant to the VWP were not included in the initial implementation but were added as of October 2004. However, Canadians and VWP country applicants for admission to the United States in a status requiring a visa (such as those with the intent to earn money in the United States) are required to enroll in US-VISIT.[7]

Given the legislation and directives, US-VISIT has clear and broad objectives. DHS states that the system will be designed to

1.  Collect, maintain, and share information, including biometric identifiers, through a dynamic system, on foreign nationals to determine whether the individual
    a.  should be prohibited from entering the United States
    b.  can receive, extend, change, or adjust immigration status
    c.  has overstayed his or her visa
    d.  needs special protection/attention (e.g., a refugee)

2.  Enhance traffic flow for individuals entering or exiting the United States for legitimate purposes by
    a.  facilitating travel and commerce
    b.  respecting the environment
    c.  strengthening international cooperation
    d.  respecting privacy laws and policies.[8]

---

Act (VWPPA), Public Law 106-396, on October 30, 2000. Public Law 104-208 (the IIRIRA) amended the statutory language to permit the Attorney General, after consultation with the Secretary of State, to determine the countries for which visas are waived. There is a requirement that aliens denied admission to the United States under the VWP must obtain a visa prior to again seeking admission.

[6]  See U.S. Department of State, Bureau of Consular Affairs, "New Requirements for Travelers" (undated).

[7]  The following visa categories are exempt from enrollment in US-VISIT: A-1 (ambassadors; public ministers; career, diplomatic, or consular officers; and members of their immediate families); A-2 (other foreign government officials or employees and members of their immediate families); C-3 (in-transit foreign government officials and members of their immediate families but not their attendants, servants, or personal employees); G-1 (principal resident representatives of recognized foreign member governments to international organizations and members of their immediate families); G-2 (other representatives of recognized foreign member governments to international organizations and members of immediate families); G-3 (representatives of non-recognized or nonmember governments to international organizations, and members of their immediate families); G-4 (international organization officers or employees and members of their immediate families); and NATO-1, NATO-2, NATO-3, NATO-4, NATO-5, and NATO-6 (representatives of NATO member countries, their dependents, clerical staff, qualified experts, and family members). However, if an individual entering the United States in an exempt status is no longer in such status on his or her date of departure, he or she would be subject to the departure requirements of his or her current status. Children under the age of 14 and persons over the age of 79 on the date of admission are exempt from US-VISIT, as are classes of aliens jointly exempted by the Secretary of Homeland Security and the Secretary of State jointly exempt. The Secretary of Homeland Security, the Secretary of State, or the Director of Central Intelligence may also exempt an individual alien. See U.S. Citizenship and Immigration Services (2005a, 2005b).

[8]  See U.S. Department of Homeland Security, "Fact Sheet: US-VISIT Program" (undated).

## The US-VISIT Process

As currently envisioned, the US-VISIT program will have four key functions, illustrated in Figure 2.1. The prime contract for building the US-VISIT system was awarded on May 28, 2004, to Accenture, LLP. The initial implementation of US-VISIT is phased and addresses the first two functions: pre-entry and entry. Entry control originally included an initial mandate that machine-readable passports be available in VWP countries by October 1, 2007. However, the Border Security Act of 2002 pushed the deadline forward to October 26, 2004; subsequent delays moved the deadline to October 26, 2005.[9] In essence, on or after October 26, 2005, any alien applying for admission under the VWP must present a passport that is tamper-resistant, machine-readable, and that uses International Civil Aviation Organization (ICAO)–

**Figure 2.1**
**Diagram of the US-VISIT Process**

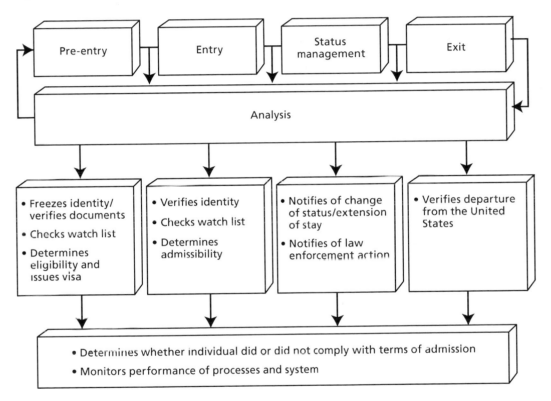

SOURCE: Adapted from Rosenberg (2004).
**RAND** *OP140-2.1*

---

9  "Biometric readers that will read ICAO [International Civil Aviation Organization] standard passports have not been deployed to U.S. ports of entry. In addition, due to technical challenges facing VWP countries in issuing their nationals machine-readable, biometric passports in compliance with standards established by ICAO, DHS requested an extension . . . to October 26, 2005" (U.S. Department of Homeland Security, Office of the Inspector General, 2005).

compliant biometric identifiers (unless the unexpired passport was issued prior to that date) (Seghetti, 2004). By the end of December 2004, US-VISIT was extended to ports of entry at the 50 busiest land borders in the United States; the system is to be operational at the remaining land borders by the end of December 2005.

## The Components and Structure of US-VISIT

### Enrollment

Visa holders enroll in US-VISIT in two ways: through a consular post or at a port of entry. Enrollment at the consular post occurs when the holder's biometric visa is processed.[10] A digital photograph of the applicant is taken, and inkless fingerprints of both index fingers are made. Then the biometric information is checked through and recorded in the IDENT (Automated Biometric Identification System) database. The State Department was required to start issuing these visas at all 211 consular posts by October 26, 2004.[11]

Alternatively, visa holders can enroll in US-VISIT at U.S. ports of entry. Initially, non-immigrant visa holders were enrolled only if they entered the United States through the 115 airports and 14 seaports that have a US-VISIT capability; as of the end of 2004, US-VISIT enrollment was also implemented at the 50 biggest land ports of entry. Here, US-VISIT is incorporated in the primary inspection performed by a U.S. Customs and Border Protection (CBP) officer.[12] The Consular Consolidated Database (CCD) is available during the primary inspection so that its contents can be compared with the passport's visa page.

When a traveler is enrolled at a port, his or her travel documents are scanned, and a digital photograph and inkless fingerprints of both index fingers are taken. The traveler's name is checked (as text, not in concert with the biometrics) against the Interagency Border Inspection System (IBIS) database and the National Crime Information Center (NCIC) database.[13]

---

[10] The mandate for a biometric passport is in Section 303 of the Enhanced Border Security and Visa Entry Reform Act of 2002. Specifically, the statute requires that all persons entering under the VWP must have such a passport if the passport was issued after October 1, 2004 (to comply with the ICAO standard of 10-year passport validity). Since there was no ICAO standard for this type of passport, often called an e-passport, ICAO had to put standards and recommendations in place for both biometrics and the appropriate "e-technology." To date, the biometric standard is a photograph suitable for facial recognition and a chip embedded in the passport; such a standard has been adopted by the United States (U.S. Department of State, Bureau of Consular Affairs, "The U.S. Electronic Passport," undated). The ICAO put forth its standards and recommendations in the summer of 2004, so VWP countries sought an extension of two years; Congress authorized only a one-year extension. The biometric of choice is the fingerprint scan.

[11] See Jacobs (2004), Congressional Testimony by the Deputy Assistant Secretary of State for Visa Services Janice Jacobs.

[12] The officers at the ports of entry are CBP officers. U.S. Immigration and Customs Enforcement (ICE) is the "interior" immigration enforcement arm; it maintains control of the SEVIS database. U.S. Citizenship and Immigration Services (USCIS) is the organization that provides benefits (e.g., adjustments to lawful permanent resident status, naturalization, or asylum) and is the owner of the Computer-Linked Application Information Management System (CLAIMS) database.

[13] IBIS contains certain terrorist watch list information from the TIPOFF database maintained by the U.S. Department of State. TIPOFF contains more than 110,000 names of known and suspected terrorists.

The combined data collection, database query, and response times are reported to take 15–23 seconds,[14] since only two fingerprints are collected and the fingerprint scans are compared only with the watch list of known or suspected violators (which is a proper subset of all stored fingerprints). In addition, within the same time frame, a one-to-one verification of biometric data is performed if the person was encountered previously at a port of entry (POE) or consular post since the inception of US-VISIT. Currently, a one-to-one verification is performed only if the stored biometric record can be accessed with the biographic data obtained from a travel document. However, the verification is not always successful; even if the person was previously enrolled by US-VISIT, the data captured from the travel document may not match exactly the data associated with the biometric record when it was initially captured (sometimes resulting in more than one biometric record per person). Although a comparison with all 10 fingerprints could mitigate this problem, current technology requires substantial time to perform a one-to-many search against all stored biometric records. Both technology and resource limitations make infeasible a search comparing the live-captured prints against all previously captured fingerprints.[15]

### Exit

The latter stages of US-VISIT are currently being designed. Exit control is particularly challenging since, unlike those in other countries, most American airports, railway stations, and border posts do not have physical space allocated for exit-control activities.

At present, it is expected that visa holders will be required to use US-VISIT to document biometrically their departure if they leave the United States using an airport or seaport that has a US-VISIT exit function. As of this writing, only Baltimore-Washington International Airport in Baltimore, Md.; airports in Dallas, Chicago, Denver, Detroit, Fort Lauderdale-Hollywood, Atlanta, Newark, Philadelphia, San Francisco, Seattle-Tacoma, and San Juan (Puerto Rico); and the Miami, Long Beach, and San Pedro passenger seaports have exit capabilities. The exit stations are self-service kiosks that resemble a bank's automated teller machines. The kiosks are to be located in the secure area of the airport, with attendants assigned to monitor the area and offer assistance. It is expected that the entry-exit information will be updated in real time; if a visitor overstays the allotted time, the failure to depart will be noted in US-VISIT.

## Using the Framework for Analysis

Although US-VISIT is not yet complete, the framework presented here for evaluating it can be applied to current and pending stages of implementation and functionality, offering not only an analysis of the pros and cons of the existing system but also suggesting ways to address issues in the unimplemented functionality.

---

[14] U.S. Department of Homeland Security, Office of the Inspector General (2005).

[15] For a discussion of the adequacy of the current (as of this writing) two-fingerprint system, see O'Harrow and Higham (2004).

Fundamentally, US-VISIT is a data collection and verification system designed to track the entry and exit of aliens to the United States. As noted above, a CBP inspector scans one or more travel documents and collects biometric data from a visitor requesting entry into the United States. Using a workstation connected directly to a central database, the inspector verifies the visitor's identity biometrically and checks the visitor's name against appropriate watch lists to determine if access should be granted. When implemented in its final form, US-VISIT will also, at a minimum, verify the exit of aliens via self-serve kiosks and double-check their information against electronically provided carrier manifest data.

From a technological standpoint, US-VISIT's proper operation relies on seven interdependent databases maintained by various government agencies. Figure 2.2 depicts the data flow and processes inherent in US-VISIT, illustrating the system's complexities. Notice that the time spent processing a nonimmigrant visitor's information may now be increased slightly by the biometric data collection and electronic verification involved.

US-VISIT is itself part of a much larger system, and its interaction with other systems raises issues about changes to system goals and functionality. For example, in August 2002, the U.S. Department of Justice published the final rule implementing the National Security Entry-Exit Registration System (NSEERS), thereby approving the fingerprinting and photographing of certain aliens, whose the fingerprints and identities would be checked against terrorist watch lists. The aliens covered by the program were a small but significant segment of those entering the country: males originating from Afghanistan, Bangladesh, Egypt, Eritrea, Indonesia, Iran, Iraq, Jordan, Kuwait, Lebanon, Libya, Morocco, North Korea, Oman, Pakistan, Qatar, Saudi Arabia, Somalia, Sudan, Syria, Tunisia, United Arab Emirates, and Yemen (Masuda, Funai, Eifert and Mitchell, Ltd., 2003). The program also required these aliens to appear periodically in person to confirm their whereabouts in the United States. On December 2, 2003, the Department of Justice suspended the 30-day re-registration and annual interview provisions of NSEERS (U.S. Department of Homeland Security, 2003b). US-VISIT now collects fingerprints and photographs from a much broader segment of nonimmigrant aliens than NSEERS does and then compares them against the IBIS watch list; NSEERS may eventually be superceded by US-VISIT when the latter is completely implemented.

A Government Accountability Office (GAO) report (Hite, 2004b) investigating US-VISIT's project management, oversight, and system acquisition issues approved the system design in general, given the short time frame for the first increment of development and deployment. However, the GAO criticized DHS for many management- and acquisition-related issues. The report points out that two of the principal challenges regarding US-VISIT's ability to meet its goals are data integrity and communication among the component databases. The seven component databases that interface with US-VISIT originally were developed to serve different purposes. The government maintains them to different standards than those of the US-VISIT system.[16] The different standards for maintaining and updating the databases that interface with US-VISIT should be rectified in subsequent phases of US-VISIT.

---

[16] Appendix A, derived from that GAO report, names the component databases, their data owners, and other details with respect to the integration with US-VISIT.

Figure 2.2
Schematic Diagram of US-VISIT Component Systems and Processes as It Currently Operates

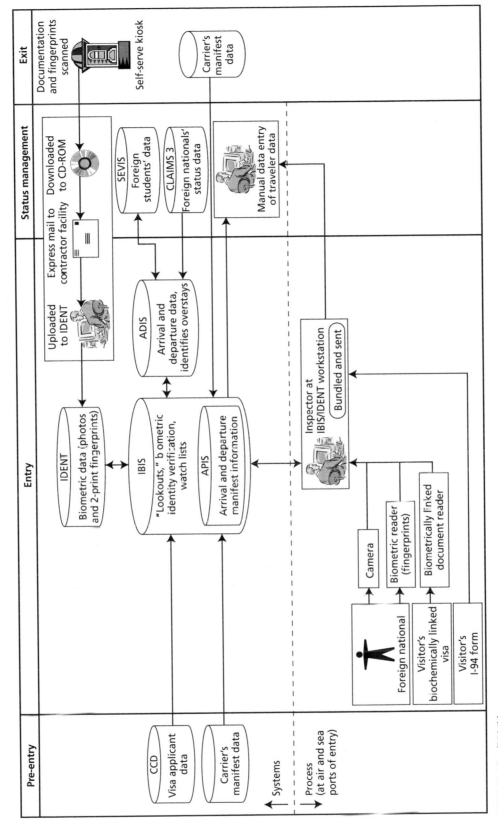

## Component System Issues

### Time Sensitivity of Data

For US-VISIT to meet its goals, it requires timely updates of information. A visitor's first encounter with US-VISIT may not be particularly time-sensitive. The pre-entry process begins when a nonimmigrant alien applies for a visa, typically months before a trip to the United States.[17] The CCD contains consular data on visa applications, approvals, and refusals, as well as the biometric identifiers captured during the process of issuance that will be compared with a traveler's documentation on arrival in the United States;[18] these data are transmitted to the US-VISIT system. Table 2.1 lists the approximate latency of data in the component databases. Therefore, the complete records are available to US-VISIT weeks or months in advance of a traveler's arrival in the United States. When the traveler books passage on a sea or air carrier, travel is typically planned at least several days in advance (though, as in the case of visas, extraordinary circumstances may arise). The air and sea passenger data lists are completed before flight or vessel departure and provided electronically to CBP, well before arrival at a U.S. port of entry. Other databases, such as IBIS,[19] CLAIMS3,[20] SEVIS,[21] and IDENT,[22] are updated continuously as data change. Therefore, while a flight or vessel is en route, US-VISIT systems at a port of entry query IBIS, IDENT, APIS,[23] ADIS,[24] CLAIMS3, and SEVIS to prepare for alien arrivals. During an alien's visit, US-VISIT, ADIS, and SEVIS are updated to determine if he or she has violated the terms of his or her visa. For example, a violation will be detected when a student drops classes or when a visitor extends his or her stay without permission. Table 2.1 lists the approximate update requirements for component systems; it indicates when data are available to US-VISIT.

---

[17] It is hoped, of course, that overseas consulates make their best efforts at expediting visa applications and processing, and that a visa could be procured in a matter of days. However, the U.S Department of State suggests planning months in advance.

[18] See Appendix A for a description of each of the cited databases.

[19] Data in the Interagency Border Inspection System (IBIS) include biographic and biometric information on suspects and fugitives. For more details, see Appendix A.

[20] Data on legal permanent residents are collected by immigration officials and stored in the Computer-Linked Application Information Management System (CLAIMS). See Appendix A for more information.

[21] The Student and Exchange Visitor Information System (SEVIS) is used to register and track foreign students in the United States. For more information, see Appendix A.

[22] IDENT is an automated biometric identification system. For more information, see Appendix A.

[23] Data about the I-94 arrival cards are stored in the Advance Passenger Information System (APIS). See Appendix A for more information.

[24] The Arrival/Departure Information System (ADIS) is a storage and query database for air and sea passengers. See Appendix A for more information.

**Table 2.1**
**US-VISIT Component Databases and Approximate Update Time**

| Database | Approximate Anticipatory Time Before Data Are Needed by US-VISIT |
|---|---|
| CCD | Days to weeks |
| SEVIS | Weeks to months |
| CLAIMS3 | Days |
| IBIS | Days |
| APIS | Hours |
| ADIS | Days |
| IDENT | Days, weeks, or months |

At land points of entry, there is no system such as APIS to signal impending arrivals of particular travelers. Therefore, the US-VISIT system accesses component databases in real-time to check the status of each individual traveler. Many foreign visitors cross U.S. land borders for work, especially along the Mexican border. Similarly, the Canadian border sees substantial traffic. For instance, the Ambassador Bridge connecting Ontario with Michigan is an extremely busy commercial corridor. According to the *Toronto Sun*,

> The 76-year-old geriatric Ambassador Bridge handles in excess of $100 billion of trade annually. This is one-quarter of the entire U.S./Canada trade. Estimates are that 40% of all truck shipments to Canada come across the Ambassador Bridge. About 10,000 trucks a day cross over both ways. (Ryan, 2005)

Community groups along the border have warned that any delays at regular, legal border crossings, whether during normal operation or when the system is malfunctioning, will create severe economic disruption and could encourage more people to try to enter illegally. Such concerns about border crossings are typical. In addition to the challenges facing entry processing, at this time it is not clear how to perform exit processing at land ports.

### Data Correctness

The multiple systems that feed US-VISIT receive their data from a variety of sources. For example, secondary schools, colleges, and universities update and manage data in SEVIS. Similarly, airline manifests feed data to APIS and ADIS. With seven connected databases and a variety of sources supplying data, the risk is high that data will be input improperly or inconsistently. Moreover, data can become corrupted due to program flaws, network malfunctions, security breaches, and a variety of other causes. Thus, it is imperative that US-VISIT checks the data, both as they are input and as they are produced by the system, to reduce the likelihood of errors.

## Algorithm Correctness

At the same time, algorithms must be checked in at least two ways: to determine that matching or forecasting algorithms are appropriate for the way in which they are used, and to verify that they have been properly implemented.

## System Redress

In spite of verification and validation procedures, some US-VISIT errors may be unavoidable. Those visitors who experience negative effects from these errors, such as undue delays or incorrect refusal to be admitted to the United States, must have speedy, effective avenues for redress. Attempts to reduce the false positive rate for identification and selection of risky visitors can lead to unacceptable rates of false negatives. US-VISIT must be monitored to help immigration officials find a balance that does not damage trade, tourism, or international cooperation.

# Deployment Schedule and Metrics of Success

The Department of Homeland Security is implementing US-VISIT incrementally. Of the four increments defined by DHS, Increments 1 through 3 are characterized as interim solutions, and the fourth increment implements the undefined final vision of US-VISIT (Hite, 2004b). Table 2.2 summarizes the characteristics of each increment, the classes of aliens covered in each increment, and the approximate number of annual aliens to be included.

**Table 2.2**
**US-VISIT Increments and Deployment Schedule**

| Increment: Date | Characteristics | Alien Classes Covered |
|---|---|---|
| 1: 01/05/2004 | The electronic collection and verification of biographic and biometric data for foreign travelers arriving with nonimmigrant visas at all major air and select sea ports of entry.[a] | Most foreign visitors seeking admission to the United States on nonimmigrant visas. |
| 2A: 10/26/2004 | The ability to process machine-readable visas and other travel and entry documents that use biometric identifiers at all ports of entry. | Foreign nationals enrolled in the Visa Waiver Program are no longer exempt and need to adhere to US-VISIT guidelines.[b] |
| 2B: 12/31/2004 | Will extend the capability of Increment 1 to the 50 highest-volume land ports of entry. | Issues surrounding the applicability of the program to Mexican and Canadian temporary visitors remain to be resolved. |
| 3: 12/31/2005 | Will extend the capability of Increment 2B to all remaining land ports of entry. | |
| 4: TBD | Yet-to-be-defined end vision of US-VISIT. | |

SOURCE: Hite (2004b).

[a] Increment 1 delivered initial operating entry capabilities to 115 airports and 14 seaports on January 5, 2004. On this day, biometric exit procedures were deployed as a pilot project at one air and one sea port of entry.
[b] U.S. biometric travel documents, following ICAO standards, will be issued to all countries in order to facilitate the processing capabilities of Increment 2A. At this time, all VWP applicants must also have machine-readable passports in compliance with ICAO standards. This phase was scheduled for implementation on October 26, 2004, but has been delayed until October 26, 2005.

A 2004 GAO report criticized the DHS for the metrics proposed to judge the success of the program (Hite, 2004b). In particular, DHS has not yet defined performance standards to assess the success of the increments. The performance metrics that have been defined include requirements for 99.5-percent system availability and the need for any relevant data to be uploaded to the system within 24 hours of the instigating event, such as the issuance of a visa. For more general performance characteristics, DHS lags in defining performance metrics and their targets. For example, GAO observed that there is no planned performance metric to assess whether the system meets the stated goal of "reduction in foreign nationals remaining in the country under unauthorized circumstances" (Hite, 2004b).

# CHAPTER THREE

# Case Study: Immigration Reform in France in the 1980s and 1990s

The use of visa restrictions to address the threat of terrorism is not new. In the 1980s, France was threatened by terrorism and reacted by tightening its border requirements. Predictions about the effects on trade, tourism, and the general good will resulting from the restrictions were similar to those voiced today in the United States. Thus, examining the relatively recent visa requirements imposed by France offers an opportunity to learn from a situation similar to that of the United States with respect to terrorism and border control.

Hollifield (1997) points out that in many ways France and the United States have had similar views about immigration. France has a long tradition of immigration, starting with the Revolution in 1789, and it was the first European state to grant citizenship to Jews. It granted citizenship based on birthright, rather than on the blood-relation required by countries such as Germany.

> For much of the post–World War II period, French governments of the Fourth and Fifth Republics pursued expansive immigration policies, essentially for three reasons. The first justification—as can be seen in the various five-year Plans—was primarily economic. During the period of reconstruction of the 1950s and 1960s (sometimes referred to as the *trente glorieuses*, or thirty glorious years of economic growth and low unemployment), France, like Germany, was in desperate need of labor. The second rationale for an open and legal immigration policy was the longstanding desire to boost the French population. Having gone through its demographic transition much earlier than other industrial societies, France was believed to have a huge demographic deficit and immigration was seen as one way to overcome this weakness. Finally, . . . policy makers and politicians had great confidence in the ability of French society to absorb and integrate the newcomers, because of the strength of the republican tradition. Therefore, an expansive, legal immigration policy was coupled with the most liberal naturalization policy in Europe, quite similar in many ways to that of the United States. (Hollifield, 1997)

However, open immigration became less popular in the early 1970s, when four characteristics of the French Republic changed. First, a recession set in and as a result, the economy could not as easily absorb newcomers as unemployment increased. Second, a flood of immigrants from many formerly French colonies, particularly Algeria, ensued as independence was granted or grabbed; these events changed the nature of the immigrant population in France.[1] Third, with the "electoral breakthrough of [Jean-Marie Le Pen of the French National Front party], a neofascist, xenophobic, and racist movement profoundly changed the politics of immigration, not only in France but throughout Western Europe" (Hollifield 1997).[2] And fourth, the 1970s and early 1980s saw an increase in terrorist activity throughout Europe, some of it perpetrated by nationalist movements (such as Basque terrorists); other incidents were orchestrated by Middle Eastern (e.g., Syrian, Iranian, and Lebanese) and North African (e.g., Algerian and Libyan) activists. Initially, some observers thought France seemed willing to allow terrorists to operate on French soil, as long as the incidents occurred elsewhere: "[T]he government reportedly worked out a *modus vivendi* with Middle Eastern terrorist groups stipulating that they could use French territory with impunity so long as no attacks took place on French soil" ("The Terrorists of France: Editorial," 1986). However, after a series of terrorist bombings in Paris killed 11 people and wounded more than 160 others, the French government took action in September 1986.

## French Action in Response to Terrorism

Passing what is commonly known as the first Pasqua Law,[3] the French government declared that visitors from countries other than those of the European Community, Liechtenstein, Monaco, Andorra, and Switzerland were required to have visas. The initial six-month requirement was extended and made permanent in 1987 (Hess, 1987). On the other hand, visas were not required for Moroccans, Tunisians, and Algerians, whose countries are former French colonies. That decision was purely economic and logistical: A French official, noting that millions of citizens from the three countries enter and leave France each year, said, "We would have to hire hundreds of extra police just to issue such visas, and frankly, we need [them] for other tasks" (Miller, 1986).

At the same time, the 12 nations belonging to the European Community convened a meeting in London of their interior and justice ministers to discuss ways to address the terrorism problem. In addition to pledging to "make effective use of existing exclusion and expulsion procedures," they urged a review of visa and extradition procedures, airport security, and "measures to curb abuses of diplomatic immunity" (Brown, 1986).

Border control was a serious issue for France. It has almost a thousand border-crossing points. Although France deployed 1,500 soldiers along its borders in 1986, many remote areas of the frontier remained unprotected ("France Hit by Visa Control Backlash," 1986). The

---

[1]  Previously, the source of much of the immigration was from nearby Catholic countries, such as Italy, Spain, and Portugal.

[2]  This action coincided with President Ronald Reagan's general amnesty for illegal immigrants in the United States in 1986, an attempt to stem the flow of immigration during a recession.

[3]  After Charles Pasqua, French Interior Minister under President François Mitterand, from 1986 to 1988. He served again as Interior Minister in the 1990s under President Edouard Balladur and instituted a second "Pasqua Law" aimed at restricting immigration.

French visa requirement for American visitors was removed in 1989 in reciprocity for participation in the VWP, but its effects offer an example of the impact of border control on trade, tourism, national security, international cooperation, and other concerns expressed about US-VISIT. In the remainder of this chapter, we examine the impact of the first Pasqua Law and assess whether the effects offer lessons for implementing US-VISIT.

## Reaction by Other Countries

As soon as the visa requirement was declared, the Council of Europe protested, calling the action by France discriminatory against eight of the 21 countries in Europe. Sweden asked the Nordic countries to debate the issue ("France Hit by Visa Control Backlash," 1986). Gabon retaliated by imposing visas for French visitors, and Senegal threatened to do the same.

By October 1986, complaints about the new visa requirement were appearing in the press. For example, the *Christian Science Monitor* reported that American visitors to France faced long lines and were angry about the visa requirements (Hess, 1987). Americans living in France found the visa process "time consuming and irritating. At first, it was unclear just what to do. Local police said it was necessary to go to the city's central police station. But at the central police station, officials said it is necessary to apply with the local police" (Echikson, 1986). Once a special visa office was established at the central railway station, no one seemed to know what was necessary for obtaining a visa.

Eventually, many of the kinks in the system were worked out. For example, an American tourist from Honolulu reported in May 1987 that "she got her visa by mail from the French consulate in San Francisco without any hardship in 10 days" (Hess, 1987). But even after several months, some problems persisted. In mid-1987, the U.S. Embassy in Paris reported that it was receiving "about four or five calls a week from American tourists blocked at airports and other border points" and that "the incidents are likely to increase" (Hess, 1987). Even at the end of the summer of 1987, "foreign embassies in Paris . . . maintained a steady stream of complaints about the bottlenecks in French consulates around the world (Graham, 1987).

French officials acknowledged early chaos but said that visa requests were being processed in only a few days, thanks to the hiring of between 600 and 1000 supplementary staff and the appropriation of 228 million French francs in special funds to computerize French consulates (Graham, 1987; Hess, 1987). They maintained that the new system, coupled with "increased police patrols, greater cooperation among international intelligence services, and French counterespionage work," was successful in discouraging terrorism (Hess, 1987).

However, travel and tourism operators were not as enthusiastic. The Chambre Nationale de la Restauration et de l'Hotellerie[4] claimed that business was down. Even French officials admitted difficulty in coping with the 4,500 Swedes who applied each day for visas during peak periods (Graham, 1987).

The psychological impact of the visa requirement was thought to be significant; a spokesperson for a Paris-based travel company noted, "It's like being put in the same bag

---

[4]    Loosely translated, the National Association of Restaurants and Hotels.

with terrorists" (Hess, 1987). Hollifield (1997) notes its effect on immigration as well: "The immediate effect of these measures was to restrict the civil liberties of foreigners, specifically North Africans, thereby launching a psychological campaign against immigrants and immigration. . . . But they also heightened the sense of crisis and contributed to the growing debate over a loss of national identity."

In 1986, tourist travel to France was down 20 percent compared to 1985, when a record number of Americans had visited. The problems seemed to persist: The number of American tourists to France in the first half of 1987 was down 35 percent from 1985, and Scandinavian charter bookings dropped 30 percent. Those numbers translate into significant financial losses: Foreign visitors spent only 66 billion French francs in 1986, compared with 71 billion in 1985 (Graham, 1987). But the downturn in tourism could easily have been attributed to other events, such as fear of terrorism or the significant decline of the U.S. dollar against the French franc. Thus, it is important to look instead at long-term tourism trends.

Foreigners, especially Arabs, expressed concern that the visa requirement might "erode the civil liberties of the more than 2 million Arab immigrant workers in France" (Echikson, 1986). A "discreet diplomatic tussle" between France and the United States, Austria, and the Nordic countries followed implementation of the visa requirement, and Norway made a formal diplomatic "demarche" to protest delays in getting visas from the French embassy in Oslo. Finland even raised concerns during a state visit by President Mitterand. Said one diplomat, "Let's face it, the measures are aimed at controlling Middle Eastern and North and West African nationals. The only reason for extending them to Americans and Europeans is so that it does not look like discrimination" (Graham, 1987). Many countries also resented the cost: sixty French francs (approximately $15) for a single entry visa, and 100 French francs for a three-year multiple-entry visa. These costs contrasted with free visas offered by the United States and some European countries, a situation no longer true today.

## Reactions Within France

Reports of French reaction are conflicting. Some articles cite early polls showing that "an overwhelming majority of the French public is willing to put up with the inconveniences" of the new policy (Echikson, 1986). But others note that the visas were unpopular because to implement the program, funds were diverted from other initiatives (Graham, 1987). Still others suggest that the visas were intended not only to control entry and exit but also to reduce immigration to zero in reaction to the changing nature of the immigrant population, particularly as expressed by Charles Pasqua (Hollifield, 1997). Indeed, Pasqua's second term, in the mid-1990s, narrowed the focus of the visa requirement: "What distinguishes this round of reform (in 1993) from earlier attempts to limit immigration (in 1974 or 1986, for example) is the clear focus on rolling back the rights of foreigners across the board" (Hollifield, 1997).[5]

In general, the French experience reflects the country's experimentation with various kinds of border controls. Traditionally, France had relied on internal labor markets to control immigration; job availability dictated who would be allowed to live and work in France. After the first Pasqua Law, these internal controls changed to external ones. As France felt the effects of stronger border control on its society and its citizens, checks and balances set in, much as they do in the United States.

> Instead of relying exclusively on the mechanism of external border controls . . . or on the more classic mechanisms of internal regulation of labor markets, the first right-wing government of the 1990s, led by Edouard Balladur, began to roll back and limit the [civil and political] rights of immigrants. . . . When the state crossed the invisible line between immigration control (on the one hand), to the point of becoming a threat to civil society and being at odds with the founding (republican) principles of the regime (on the other hand), institutional/ judicial, ideological, and social checks came into play. As in other liberal republics, immigration control in France is not purely a function of markets, economic interests, or national security. It is heavily dependent on the interplay of ideas, institutions, and civil society. (Hollifield, 1997)

## Effects on Immigration, Tourism, and Trade

It is in this context that we can examine the trends in immigration and tourism in France. Table 3.1 and Figure 3.1 show that immigration had been dropping before France implemented its visa requirement; the entire drop cannot be attributable solely to the visa requirement. It is clear from French government policy decisions that the visa requirement was only one of a number of changes designed to keep out foreign workers, especially those who did not meet a particular demographic profile. For example, "the second Pasqua Law (like the first) sought to change naturalization procedures by requiring children born in France of foreign parents to make a formal request for naturalization, between the ages of 16 and 21" (Hollifield, 1997).

---

[5]  Hollifield (1997) explores the parallel with the United States during this time period. "The debate in France over social rights for immigrants parallels a similar debate that was gathering force in the United States, especially in California, where voters approved a measure (Proposition 187) in November 1994 to cut public and social services for illegal immigrants. Barely two years later (in 1996), the U.S. Congress, under Republican control, would adopt similar laws to cut social ser- vices for legal as well as illegal immigrants, and the rights of appeal for illegals and asylum seekers would be sharply cur- tailed. Also in the U.S., proposals were made by prominent right-wing politicians, such as Governor Pete Wilson of Cali- fornia, to limit birthright citizenship, so that the children born of foreign parents would no longer be automatically entitled to American citizenship."

**Table 3.1**
**Immigration of Workers and Their Family Members to France by Year, 1982–1989**

| Population | Year | | | | | | | |
|---|---|---|---|---|---|---|---|---|
| | 1982 | 1983 | 1984 | 1985 | 1986 | 1987 | 1988 | 1989 |
| Workers | 96,962 | 18,483 | 11,804 | 10,959 | 11,238 | 12,231 | 14,594 | 18,646 |
| Seasonal workers | 107,084 | 101,857 | 93,220 | 86,180 | 81,670 | 76,647 | 70,547 | 61,868 |
| Family members | 47,366 | 45,731 | 39,586 | 32,512 | 27,116 | 26,746 | 29,345 | 34,594 |
| Total | 251,412 | 166,071 | 144,610 | 129,651 | 120,024 | 115,624 | 114,486 | 115,108 |

SOURCE: Lebon (1988, 1989, 1990).

During the same period, a decline in tourism was reported in the press. However, as indicated by Table 3.2, the decline was minimal, since overall figures show a substantial increase in tourists from year to year. What is more likely is that revenues were down in the tourist industry. The revenue decline probably resulted from tourists hesitant to spend their money in a more expensive France; the visa requirement was instituted when the French franc was strengthening considerably against the U.S. dollar.

**Figure 3.1**
**Trend in Immigration of Workers and Their Family Members to France, 1982–1989**

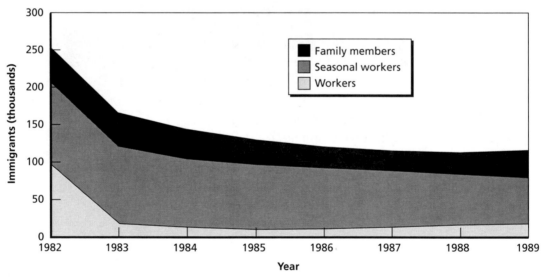

SOURCE: Lebon (1988, 1989, 1990).
RAND OP140-3.1

Table 3.2
Tourist Arrivals By Region to France, 1986–1990

| Region | Year | | | | |
|---|---|---|---|---|---|
| | 1986 | 1987 | 1988 | 1989 | 1990 |
| Americas | 2,750,000 | 2,931,000 | 3,045,000 | 3,005,000 | 3,300,000 |
| Europe | 30,959,000 | 31,749,000 | 32,778,000 | 44,074,000 | 46,835,000 |
| Asia, East and Southeast/Oceania | 800,000 | 853,000 | 950,000 | 1,033,000 | 900,000 |
| Southern Asia | 135,000 | 156,000 | 171,000 | — | — |
| Western Asia | 316,000 | 249,000 | 278,000 | 213,000 | 250,000 |
| Region not specified | — | — | 4,433,000 | 250,000 | — |
| Africa | 1,120,000 | 1,036,000 | 1,066,000 | 1,583,000 | 1,500,000 |
| Total | 36,080,000 | 36,974,000 | 42,721,000 | 50,158,000 | 52,785,000 |

SOURCE: United Nations Statistics Division, Common Database.

NOTE: Statistics for the years cited in the table are no longer available from the United Nations Statistics Division Common Database. For these statistics for the years 1999 to 2003, see United Nations Statistics Division (undated).

Table 3.3 illustrates that, despite the possible downturn in tourist income, the general trade picture in France from 1985 to 1990 was still healthy. Thus, the visa requirement seems not to have had any significant negative impact on French trade.

Although the French visa requirement was lifted for Americans in 1989 as the Visa Waiver Program was instituted, a French visa is still required for travelers from many other countries. There are no reports of long-term negative effects from the visa requirement on French national security or international cooperation.

Table 3.3
Total Import and Export Value (in U.S. Dollars) for France, 1985–1990

| Activity | Year | | | | | |
|---|---|---|---|---|---|---|
| | 1985 | 1986 | 1987 | 1988 | 1989 | 1990 |
| Imports | 108,379 | 129,435 | 158,499 | 177,288 | 190,963 | 233,207 |
| Exports | 101,709 | 124,863 | 148,402 | 167,813 | 173,073 | 210,169 |

SOURCE: United Nations (1993).

## Lessons Learned from the French Experience

There are many clear parallels between France's actions in 1986 and U.S. actions today. Imposition of a visa requirement in France seems to have had no long-term negative economic impact on trade and tourism, despite predictions of dire consequences. The international community seems to have understood that a trade-off must be made between free access and national security. Nevertheless, the visa requirement led to a clear initial drop in immigration that persisted for several years. Similar drops may be less desirable in the United States, particularly for seasonal workers and students. The effects of the French visa requirements were felt in the context of a larger, and intentionally restrictive, immigration policy; US-VISIT's effects must be viewed in the same larger context, with reasoned consideration of what the United States would like to accomplish with immigration and border controls.

# CHAPTER FOUR

# Policy Issues Related to US-VISIT

As noted earlier, overall border control is a daunting task. US-VISIT supports border control by aiding the identification and monitoring of nonimmigrant aliens visiting the United States, it is only one of a range of programs to control alien access to the country. Its exclusive focus is the legal process enabling foreigners to visit the United States; it does not attempt to resolve many of the issues related to illegal immigration. In this section, we identify fundamental policy issues related to the US-VISIT program. The discussion is tied to the US-VISIT stages through which a nonimmigrant alien must pass as he or she enters, visits, and leaves the United States.

To accomplish this task, we consider the structure and processes of US-VISIT, comparing them to the goals of the program and the case study of the French response to terrorism in the 1980s and 1990s. The identification and analysis of policy issues are based on several assumptions:

- The implementation of US-VISIT will continue; it was extended to VWP countries in October 2004 and to the 50 busiest land ports of entry in 2005.
- The GAO will continue to perform a program oversight function that monitors the acquisition, deployment, and management of US-VISIT.
- The United States must balance several goals relating to trade, tourism, immigration, international cooperation, and national security.

Here, our goal is to elucidate issues directly and indirectly related to US-VISIT, not to analyze the costs and benefits of the program.

The US-VISIT program must satisfy the needs of multiple constituencies. The primary constituency is the U.S. citizenry that, by virtue of a more effective immigration system, benefits from the legitimate travel and trade of foreigners in the United States and is protected from harm that results from illegitimate travel and trade of foreigners. In addition to economic benefits, the benefits of an effective immigration system include reduced risk of terrorist attacks by foreigners, fewer visa violations, and enhanced public safety through the apprehension of foreign criminals at the border. As US-VISIT is implemented at U.S. ports of entry and departure, it will keep records of individual travelers, allowing additional scrutiny regarding their visits to the United States. In general, to the majority of U.S. citizens, the benefits of US-VISIT are indirect.

Several constituencies bear the costs of the program. While U.S. taxpayers fund the US-VISIT program, foreign travelers are forced to submit biometric information as a condition of entering the country. Although US-VISIT has not increased processing times at the border appreciably, visitors are affected by more than the possibility of increased waiting times. The biographic and biometric information collected as part of the visa issuance and entrance processes is checked against criminal watch lists for all visitors, even absent admission. Additionally, as US-VISIT builds a database of entrances and exits, threats to travelers' personal privacy loom.[1] Since foreign travelers bear the majority of the social costs of the US-VISIT program, one would hope that implementation details of the US-VISIT program at the border would acknowledge the disparity between groups bearing the cost and those reaping the benefits.[2]

Attention surrounding US-VISIT has been focused on its technological components. Each immigration officer has a digital fingerprint scanner and a digital camera with which to capture photographs, and a workstation connected to local and remote databases (including law enforcement, DOS, and CBP systems). The GAO reviews of the system have focused on system availability and processes. Metrics of system performance are also technological and include system availability and query response time.

The technological focus raises many questions. First, the US-VISIT system is not simply a system for collecting and organizing visitors' pictures and fingerprints. Rather, it is a component of a broader system to enforce U.S. immigration law. One of its functions is to check foreign visitors against criminal and terrorist watch lists. However, the processes and procedures for maintaining these watch lists vary considerably. Moreover, the agencies that maintain the watch lists, enroll students, and issue visas are not the agencies responsible for border enforcement. Intended initially for narrow purposes, the watch lists and systems were not necessarily designed for broader applicability. Therefore, the ultimate success of US-VISIT depends in part on the ability of CBP border inspectors to coordinate their processes and requirements with those agencies on whose data they rely.

Table 4.1 illustrates the direct and indirect policy issues raised by US-VISIT based on the program processes.

Using the table, we can group US-VISIT policy issues in five areas: information technology and information security; personal privacy and data correctness; organizational coordination; travel, trade, and tourism; and national security, as shown in Table 4.2. Following the table are general recommendations for monitoring and minimizing the negative effects of each of these issues as US-VISIT continues to be implemented.

---

[1]    However, travelers normally expect records of their border crossings to be maintained by foreign governments.

[2]    The increased security that is claimed to be provided by US-VISIT would seem to benefit U.S. citizens and foreigners equally. However, we do not know the extent to which foreigners are a danger to other foreigners on U.S. soil.

**Table 4.1**
**Identification of US-VISIT Policy Issues Based on Analysis of the US-VISIT Process**

| US-VISIT Process | Directly Related Policy Issues | Indirectly Related Policy Issues |
|---|---|---|
| Pre-entry | • DOS/DHS coordination<br>• Availability of consular services and resources<br>• Non-VWP and VWP parity<br>• Secure communication and data transmission<br>• Safeguarding personal privacy<br>• Access to system | • Foreign educational opportunity<br>• Encouragement of trade and tourism<br>• Limiting access to dangerous individuals |
| Entry | • Query speed and response accuracy<br>• System availability<br>• Access to system<br>• System reliability, including minimization of false positives and negatives<br>• Redress processes at the border<br>• Canada and Mexico parity<br>• Coordination of databases<br>• Safeguarding personal privacy<br>• Alternate entry points | • Denying access to dangerous individuals<br>• Implementation schedule<br>• Impact on trade and tourism |
| Status management | • Data quality and timeliness<br>• Coordination with law enforcement and other agencies, and educational institutions | • Tracking alien movements<br>• Authority and processes for expulsion |
| Exit | • Availability of facilities at ports<br>• Availability of exit services<br>• Process change<br>• Query speed and response accuracy<br>• System availability<br>• Coordination with status management<br>• Public/private data coordination | • Facilitating future legal visits to the United States<br>• Implementation schedule<br>• Investment and funding |

## Information Technology and Information Security

Central to the US-VISIT program are the development and implementation of databases of traveler information and user interfaces to facilitate collection and retrieval of data. Effective operation of US-VISIT requires a robust system that is reliable and secure. The performance of the US-VISIT technology will have a direct effect on the encouragement of legitimate trade and tourism and the discouragement of improper access to the country. If US-VISIT were difficult to use and failure prone, it would discourage legitimate travel to the United States. Likewise, if US-VISIT were ineffective in identifying and apprehending dangerous individuals, it would not protect Americans and their guests, regardless of ease of use. To avoid these situations, we suggest several policies that encourage the information technology to function appropriately.

**Table 4.2**
**General Policy Areas and Issues Related to US-VISIT**

| Policy Area | Policy Issues |
| --- | --- |
| Information technology and information security | • System reliability—component and overall<br>• System access rules<br>• User interface design and testing<br>• Communication links and remote access<br>• System mobility<br>• Tamper-resistance/tamper-evidence<br>• Public oversight |
| Personal privacy and data correctness | • Traveler access to data<br>• Data creation, retention, and destruction<br>• Rules for data correction<br>• Responsibility for data maintenance<br>• System changes, upgrades, and opportunity for discussion of privacy issues<br>• Public oversight |
| Interagency coordination | • Information updates<br>• Responsibility for data updates and correctness<br>• Process for notification of violators<br>• Process for error resolution<br>• System maintenance |
| Travel, trade, and tourism | • Availability of consular services<br>• System flexibility<br>• Outreach and foreign education of US-VISIT goals and benefits<br>• Educational opportunity<br>• Reciprocity of foreign governments<br>• Ease of redress |
| National security | • Identification/apprehension of dangerous individuals<br>• Coordination with other nations<br>• Shift to alternate means of entering United States |

## System Reliability

There are many actions that can be taken to ensure system reliability, ranging from formal specification of requirements and design to Failure Modes and Effects Analysis (FMEA) (O'Connor, 2002). The implementers of US-VISIT should create an in-depth quality assurance policy whose enforcement would, at the very least:

- Identify ways in which the system might fail, and then design and implement strategies for mitigating each failure mode.
- Define test suites to ensure that any changes to the system preserve functionality and performance while testing new features and enhancements.
- Address issues of software integration, especially when parts of the system are acquired from other sources.
- Define measures of system success and apply them to monitor false positives and negatives, system availability, and system use.

### User Interface Design and Testing

Users such as immigration officers should not be expected to be software experts. The user interface must be designed and tested to ensure that errors are not introduced because of ambiguity or confusion about what the system does and how it does works. In particular, a well-designed user interface offers several advantages, including reduced training time, speed of processing, reduction in human error, and compliance with policy. That is, the interface should be designed so that the user can most easily complete routine tasks; progressively more training may be needed to learn to complete complicated tasks. The US-VISIT interfaces, which include user interfaces to all component databases such as CCD, IBIS, ADIS, SEVIS, and CLAIMS3, demand extra attention to the tasks that CBP inspectors perform on a routine basis: scanning and validating documents, collecting photographs and fingerprints, and querying IBIS regarding applicants' admissibility status. The interfaces should also limit personal information disclosure only to authorized individuals. US-VISIT contractors should work with users and stakeholders—the alien applicants—to ensure that the data input, retrieval, and correction processes are seamless and error-free.

### Communication Links

In Chapter Two, Figure 2.2 illustrates the component systems and connections of US-VISIT. Each of the links in the diagram depicts an electronic data connection, except for the exit-kiosks, from which data are transferred manually on a daily basis. Table 2.1 lists the approximate data-time-sensitivity of the component databases. Despite the latency of several of the databases, proper operation of the US-VISIT system requires that the communication links be available at all times and have several other properties, all of which should be subject to independent verification and monitoring:

- *Secure.* The communications between systems must be secure. A query from an IBIS/IDENT terminal operated by a CBP officer must have a secure connection to the IBIS mainframe that returns the results. To our knowledge, the US-VISIT suite of systems has these properties, communicating among one another through encrypted Internet links.
- *Redundant.* No communication link is completely reliable, but because legal immigration to the United States will soon rely entirely on the proper operation of US-VISIT, it is essential that the links among the terminals and databases be functionally redundant. To achieve this state, it will be critical that the designers of the final US-VISIT version perform FMEA to predict and obviate communication failures. A redundant system may require frequent backup and remote storage of US-VISIT data in addition to multiple communication paths.
- *Traceable.* Because US-VISIT component systems transmit and receive personal information critical to the enforcement of U.S. immigration law and possibly critical to protecting U.S. national security, it is imperative that communications among systems be logged and recorded with information that identifies users. Periodic audits of log files should be performed. These properties will allow DHS to monitor the operation of the system to guarantee against fraud and abuse.

## Personal Privacy and Data Correctness

US-VISIT is designed not only to interact with many databases but also to amalgamate information from them and make judgments, such as when visitors are flagged as terrorists or criminals. Information captured for one purpose in one part of the network may be used for a very different purpose by another part of the network. Thus, privacy concerns are paramount and must be addressed and revisited as the system expands and its data are made available to other systems.

Privacy policies and considerations have evolved with the expanding use of networked personal data. In 1972, the Advisory Committee on Automated Data Systems was created through the U.S. Department of Health, Education, and Welfare with the charge to "analyze harmful consequences that might result from automated personal data systems" (Ware, 1973). The Advisory Committee recommended the creation of the Federal Code of Fair Information Practices. The Code of Fair Information Practices is based on five principles described in the committee's report: notice and awareness, access and participation, choice and consent, enforcement and redress, and integrity and security (U.S. Department of Health, Education, and Welfare, 1972). U.S. government agencies must adhere to the Code of Fair Information Practices. The Organization for Economic Cooperation and Development (OECD) adopted an expanded set of principles in 1980. The European Union formalized its own standard for information privacy in the "Safe Harbor" principles. The Safe Harbor principles include provisions for notice to individuals of data collection, choice by the individual, requirements for onward transfer of the data, security of the data, integrity of the data, access protocols and need-to-know, and enforcement of compliance (U.S. International Trade Administration, 1999).

The Safe Harbor principles of the OECD guidelines seem to have been the basis for the U.S. Department of Homeland Security's recently posted privacy principles, available on its US-VISIT Web site.[3] These principles address many of the same issues, as illustrated in Table 4.3.

These principles are accompanied by a privacy policy to explain who will have access to collected data, how the data will be used, how long data will be retained, and how to implement the redress procedures.[4] US-VISIT has a privacy officer responsible for implementing the principles and policies. Given the millions of visitors to the United States who will be subject to inspection via US-VISIT, maintaining the principles of the privacy policy will be a difficult and persistent challenge.

---

[3] See U.S. Department of Homeland Security, "US-VISIT Privacy Principles" (undated).

[4] See U.S. Department of Homeland Security, "US-VISIT Privacy Policy" (undated).

**Table 4.3**
**US-VISIT Privacy Principles**

| Principle | Description |
|---|---|
| Responsibility and accountability | All US-VISIT personnel and users are responsible and accountable for treating personal information in accordance with these principles. The US-VISIT Privacy Officer is ultimately responsible and accountable for compliance with these principles, including the safeguarding of personal information. |
| Privacy awareness and training | US-VISIT personnel and contractors will be appropriately educated and trained regarding the proper treatment of personal information. |
| Openness and redress | US-VISIT will make its privacy policy and practices readily available to individuals and provide a complaint and redress process. |
| Identifying purpose | The purposes for which personal information is collected will be identified by US-VISIT at or before the time of collection. |
| Informed consent | Individuals will be informed of and allow the collection, use, and disclosure of their personal information. |
| Limiting collection, use, disclosure, and retention | The collection, use, disclosure, and retention of personal information will be limited to that which is necessary for the stated purposes of US-VISIT. |
| Strict confidentiality | Personal information will only be disclosed to authorized individuals with a legitimate need to know, and only for uses that are consistent with the stated purposes for which the information was collected. |
| Data integrity | US-VISIT will maintain the accuracy, completeness, and currency of personal information at levels necessary for the stated purposes of US-VISIT. |
| Individual access | Upon request, individuals will have their records accessed, reviewed, and corrected, as needed, to ensure accuracy and completeness. |
| Security | Personal information will be protected by administrative, technical, and physical safeguards appropriate to the sensitivity of the information. |

SOURCE: U.S. Department of Homeland Security, "US-VISIT Privacy Principles" (undated).

## Interagency Coordination

A set of policy issues regarding US-VISIT is derived from the information-sharing requirements among various public- and private-sector organizations. Timely and accurate information-sharing is absolutely critical to the success of the US-VISIT program. Figure 4.1 depicts a simple network map illustrating the connections among the major public and private organizations that feed into US-VISIT; the network map illustrates the agencies and individuals who must coordinate their actions for US-VISIT to operate properly.

At the center of the figure are the DHS and its agencies that are responsible for implementing immigration law and executing border regulations. The DOS issues visas, communicating with educational institutions regarding student visas and with DHS regarding the visa applications it has approved and those it has rejected. Air and sea carriers communicate passenger information to facilitate the entry and exit operations of US-VISIT. Law enforcement

**Figure 4.1**
**Network Map of the Information-Sharing Requirements**
**Among Various Government and Private-Sector Agencies**

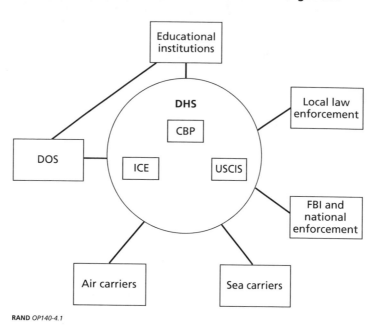

**RAND** *OP140-4.1*

agencies at all levels maintain watch lists that are provided to DHS; presumably, they are able to respond to information from DHS regarding US-VISIT participants who violate the terms of their visits to the United States. We have already discussed the information technology issues surrounding communication among systems. Here we address the organizational issues instigated by the requirement to coordinate information-sharing among such a large number of disparate players.

- *Responsibility for data updates and maintenance.* Appendix A lists the component databases used by US-VISIT and the data owners. A CBP inspector uses the system in real time to compare an applicant with the IBIS database and to verify visa status. Other agencies may or may not be required to maintain data within such short time intervals. Consular services may update visa documentation once per day, and officials at institutions that maintain foreign student status information may update the system at times commensurate with the academic calendar. Law enforcement agencies input data to watch lists at unpredictable intervals. The success of US-VISIT requires DHS to know the latency of all data on which it bases its decision to admit an alien requesting entry. DHS must also rely on the data suppliers to verify and correct data as necessary. Note that this caveat includes not only the uploading of new data but also the validation of current data. For example, the FBI may place an individual on a watch list but subsequently find the individual not to be a suspect; it is the Federal Bureau of Investigation (FBI) that is responsible for updating the information. DHS should publish publicly its rules for updating information regarding US-VISIT.

- *Responsibility for data correctness and redress.* The US-VISIT system relies on data collected and input by DHS; DOS; educational institutions; air, land and sea carriers; and law enforcement agencies. An error in any of these sources can lead a CBP inspector to reject an alien's application for entry to the United States, inadvertently affecting legitimate travel and trade. Errors in data can also lead to unauthorized acceptance of dangerous individuals, defeating the purpose of the system. Therefore, enforceable processes for ensuring data correctness are paramount. Equally important are redress processes, enabling data to be corrected by aliens or official representatives.
- *Component system availability, security, and maintenance.* Many of the systems used by US-VISIT are not under direct DHS control. For example, DOS may conclude that it needs to take the CCD offline for a short period of time for system maintenance and upgrades. Likewise, SEVIS may be unavailable as the result of the actions of hackers. There must be an agreed-upon protocol for communicating system outages and planned upgrades so that US-VISIT remains available through any contingency.

## Travel, Trade, and Tourism

From its inception through January 24, 2005, the US-VISIT system screened over 18 million travelers to the United States, leading to 2,290 matches with law enforcement databases. The matches included 1,046 criminals and 1,244 immigration violators (U.S. Department of Homeland Security, Office of the Inspector General, 2005). This hit rate of 1.27 in 10,000 has been heralded as a success by DHS. However, identification and apprehension must be balanced with possible negative effects on trade, tourism, and perceptions of privacy. For example, the DHS Inspector General's report notes that, at land ports of entry, "small increases in processing times . . . can have deleterious economic costs and effects for both border nations" (U.S. Department of Homeland Security, Office of the Inspector General, 2005). Below, we list several major issues that will allow US-VISIT to facilitate international exchange.

- *Availability of consular services.* Post–September 11, 2001, changes to visa processes require most visa applicants to apply in person at a U.S. embassy or consulate, and to submit to an interview as part of the process. In many cases, changes to a nonimmigrant's visa require application at the foreign consulate as well. This in-person requirement, although facilitating the collection of biometrics, contrasts with the French policy of issuing visas by mail. To ensure that legitimate travel and trade are encouraged, the United States should make consular services available to the broadest segment of the foreign population possible. It may be desirable to allow biometrics to be collected by designated trusted organizations not located at the consulates, while constantly seeking to increase the ability to review applications thoroughly.[5]

5 Substantial visa application fees are also being perceived as a barrier by some aliens. The $100 fee has been criticized as excessive and discouraging of travel and tourism to the United States. In retaliation, Brazil has instituted similar

- *Outreach and foreign education of US-VISIT goals and benefits.* The United States, both by proclamation and legislation, suddenly announced the US-VISIT program and its requirements for machine-readable passports with biometric identifiers. This situation left foreign governments and travelers with little time to prepare or respond. The functioning of US-VISIT could be bolstered if the United States were to plan for the eventuality of similar systems overseas. For example, the DOS began to issue machine-readable visas in 2004 based on the collection and query of fingerprint scans. However, should other countries implement similar systems, there may be a backlash among U.S. travelers. The United States has the right to set immigration laws and requirements for its visitors. However, to encourage legitimate travel and trade, it is imperative that the United States educate foreigners on the system's requirements and goals, responding sincerely to complaints as it would to stakeholders when setting national policy.

- *Fostering educational opportunity.* The DOS notes that foreign students are ultimately responsible for ensuring that their data are accurately represented in SEVIS; otherwise, their application for entry will be denied. This requirement seems reasonable but ignores the reality that many foreign students have no access to the necessary electronic and telecommunication systems; indeed, many might not have a command of English. The DOS, working with educational institutions, should institute processes that double-check the records of foreign students in SEVIS, aiding the smooth operation of the entire foreign-student system.

- *Ease of redress.* We have noted that, given the range agencies maintaining component systems of US-VISIT, it is inevitable that routine errors will occur. These errors may include the false-positive identification of a traveler as a terrorist, or the rejection of an application for entry because of a technical malfunction. The DOS and DHS should seek to ensure that the process for filing a legitimate complaint is simple and that aliens have a right to petition to correct their data prior to deportation.

- *Extension to all ports.* America's land ports of entry with Canada and Mexico are critical economic links. For example, the Ambassador Bridge between Detroit, Mich., and Windsor, Ontario, is essential for U.S. automakers, and the border crossings between Texas and Mexico provide an important source of trade and labor for the United States (Ryan, 2005). The Perryman Group (2004) studied the potential economic effect of US-VISIT based on assumptions about the delay imposed on persons and trucks. It concluded that the economic effect of full US-VISIT implementation along the Mexican border will be $61 billion and lead to the loss of over 300,000 jobs. It is essential that the implementation of US-VISIT along land ports of entry take into account the nature and function of the border economy so that trade and tourism will be minimally affected.

policies—fingerprinting and a $100 fee—for Americans seeking to visit. It is not yet known whether other countries are putting similar obstacles in place for American visitors, or whether these obstacles are likely to be short-lived.

## National Security

Although US-VISIT's legislative mandate goes back to 1996, the terrorist attacks of September 11, 2001, motivated its quick implementation. For this reason, US-VISIT is viewed primarily as a means of enhancing U.S. national security. (Indeed, only under such circumstances could a one in 10,000 "hit rate" be touted as success.) But the ability of US-VISIT, including all component systems, to protect the United States from foreign criminals will always be limited because there is no centralized means of tracking foreign movements throughout the United States. The onus is on the U.S. Department of State (when issuing visas) and on CBP inspectors (at the port of entry) to identify and reject inappropriate individuals.[6] In the event that a foreigner is suspected of committing crimes in the United States, law enforcement agencies must be able to access US-VISIT databases to retrieve biographic and biometric information. However, such access may violate an individual's privacy, so legitimate legal routes must exist. Moreover, there is a historical reluctance among federal law enforcement officials to share information with local law enforcement officers; although improving, this hesitation, added to the conflict between privacy and national security goals, limits the ability of US-VISIT to deter dangerous individuals from entering the country. Additionally, if US-VISIT evolves into an effective law enforcement tool, it may motivate dangerous individuals to seek alternative means of entering the United States, avoiding the US-VISIT system entirely.

Several other issues affect the ability of US-VISIT to improve national security.

- *Identification/apprehension of dangerous individuals.* If a person truly presents a danger to the national security of the United States, or is thought to be a foreign criminal, it is important that the person be identified to U.S. officials as early as possible in the process of seeking admission to the United States. This identification can occur overseas, when an alien applies for a visa, or at the border, during application for entry; in the case of non–visa carriers, this process will occur at the border.[7] To ensure that the process is as effective as possible, the United States should seek to coordinate its issuance of visas with foreign governments and law enforcement agencies. At the border, it is possible to perform a certain degree of pre-selection of suspect applicants by scrutinizing the air and sea carrier manifests in anticipation of arrival.
- *Tracking individuals within the United States.* When fully implemented, US-VISIT will record the arrival and departure of nonimmigrant aliens. However, the system will provide only minimal means for tracking the whereabouts of aliens while they visit the United States. Of course, commercial transactions, as well as contacts with law enforcement, provide a means of observing certain types of behavior. Therefore, it is important that the information-sharing and disclosure requirements are specified so that local law enforcement officials have the ability to access US-VISIT data under certain circumstances.

---

6   Customs and Border Protection is not the only agency responsible for identifying foreign criminals and overstayers. Immigration and Customs Enforcement has a collection of programs designed to detect unwelcome visitors. However, the CBP is most directly connected with US-VISIT and thus is the focus of discussion here.

7   Should these border protection mechanisms fail, the identification can also occur within U.S. borders, if the alien violates conditions of entry or breaks U.S. law.

- *Shift to illegal entry means.* Ironically, if US-VISIT is successful, its implementation might have the unintended consequence of motivating certain aliens to attempt to gain entry via illegal means. Therefore, it is essential that DHS balance the requirements for legal nonimmigrant aliens with more effective border policing.

# CHAPTER FIVE

# Conclusions and Recommendations for Further Inquiry

The overview of US-VISIT systems and processes, the summary of the French response to terrorism in the 1980s and 1990s, and the identification of fundamental policy issues related to US-VISIT suggest several observations and avenues for future analysis and policy.

## Creating and Maintaining a Complex System

The US-VISIT system, viewed in the context of its multiple goals, multiple sources of information, and multiple audiences for its results, is a complex and evolving system. For this reason, systems engineering provides a useful vantage point from which to view US-VISIT and examine many of its related policy issues. US-VISIT requires reliable and secure databases and communication links, coordinated updating and sharing of information among disparate government agencies, and specified processes for safeguarding personal privacy and enabling the timely correction of data. There is a need for an independent analysis of US-VISIT from a systems engineering perspective. Such an analysis would quantify the relationships among US-VISIT component systems, suggest standards for compatibility and correctness, and make explicit the responsibilities among government agencies for updating data, among other issues.

## International Privacy Considerations

The US-VISIT system collects biographic and biometric data from foreigners. Some of the data are required for entry (i.e., the photograph and fingerprint); other data are supplied by third parties. For example, air and sea carriers provide manifest data to CBP prior to the arrival of the aircraft. Because US-VISIT requires the disclosure of these data to U.S. government officials and systems, it is imperative that the program takes into account international requirements for data privacy and protection, not just U.S. norms. For example, the European Privacy Directive prohibits data from being used for a purpose other than that for which it was collected. Such privacy restrictions make it difficult for US-VISIT to collect and use personal data collected in other countries. There exists a need for an independent assessment of international privacy laws and their relationship to the development and implementation of US-VISIT.

## US-VISIT in the Broader Context of Border Control

It has always been challenging to control and protect U.S. borders, and the events of September 11, 2001, have added significantly to the challenge. Although the legal mandate for US-VISIT dates to 1996, the attacks of September 11 accelerated the need to have a more solid system in place. Thus, even though US-VISIT addresses substantial security needs, it is fundamentally a modernization of the U.S. border control system. Therefore, when evaluating US-VISIT, we must keep in mind that no border control systems, strategies, or tactics are perfect. US-VISIT is a large undertaking that requires continuous oversight and evaluation to ensure that it accomplishes its many goals. In particular, systems should be put in place to measure the degree to which US-VISIT is meeting its border control targets without diminishing U.S. capacity to welcome tourists, promote trade, and encourage international cooperation and collaboration.

## Technological and Cultural Considerations

The US-VISIT system, including all component databases, information pathways, and human interactions, eventually will automate the entry and exit process for nonimmigrant aliens. Since the system automatically checks traveler names against a range of databases, a false positive match can result in the rejection of a legitimate applicant, possibly leading to deportation and incarceration. Additionally, the collection of photographs and fingerprints could be viewed as intrusive by some cultures and religions, and might discourage the type of cultural exchange that keeps Americans connected to the world. US-VISIT should include in its subsystems a strategy for monitoring its direct and indirect effects on visitors. That is, in addition to capturing information on the number of people screened and the number of aliens denied entrance, it should also monitor visitors and trade partners to gauge their reaction to US-VISIT's enhanced scrutiny. Tables of data about U.S. revenue from foreign trade, dollars spent by foreign tourists, and numbers of foreign students studying in the United States are essential for ensuring that US-VISIT is having no unintended effects.

## Take Your Time

Critics of US-VISIT worry that the system will be only marginally effective at deterring criminals from entering the United States and will have a drastic effect on cross-border trade. When France instituted similar requirements on foreign visitors in the 1980s and 1990s, the number of foreign visitors slumped briefly, but tourism revenues quickly recovered. To date, US-VISIT has had little effect on tourism, if only because the system initially applied to a small proportion of nonimmigrant visitors.[1] As US-VISIT expands to visitors from VWP countries and to

---

[1]   Although not directly attributable to US-VISIT, the significant downturn in applications from foreigners to study in the United States has had a substantial economic impact on U.S. educational institutions.

land borders, it might significantly affect travel to and trade with the United States. France's experience tells us that we should not rush to judge US-VISIT in the short term, but rather take a measured approach that evaluates the system, its processes, and its effects over months or years. To prepare for this, DHS, DOS, educational institutions, commercial stakeholders, and tourist destinations should be prepared to measure the effects of US-VISIT through a set of quantitative metrics that indicate trends over time. In addition, these constituencies should meet periodically to address possible negative effects of US-VISIT.

# US-VISIT Component Databases

**Table A.1**
**US-VISIT Component Databases, Data Sources, and Characteristics**

| Database | Definition | Description | Data Source | Data Owner | Notes |
|---|---|---|---|---|---|
| ADIS | Arrival/ Departure Information System | Storage and query database for air and sea passengers | APIS | ICE[a] | Automatic and manual data exchange and queries with IDENT, SEVIS, and CLAIMS3<br><br>Query occurs before flight or vessel arrival to prepare CBP inspectors for the arrival of a group of aliens. |
| APIS | Advance Passenger Information System | Capture database for air and sea passengers | Air and sea carrier incoming and exit manifests | CBP | Receives incoming manifest data as flights and ships enter and leave the United States |
| IBIS | Interagency Border Inspection System | "Watch list" database including biographic and biometric information on suspects and fugitives, evidence records (i.e., fingerprints) and other information[b] | At least 30 data sources including systems such as APIS, and agencies, such as DHS (CBP and ICE), FBI, legacy INS, U.S. Secret Service, BATF,[c] Royal Canadian Mounted Police, and Interpol<br><br>In 2001, it was estimated that 30,000 people had access to IBIS.[b] | ICE and CBP[d] | Almost any law enforcement agency can submit a record to IBIS or make a query (e.g., if fingerprints are found at a crime scene, to see if the offender is wanted for immigration violations). |
| IDENT | Automated Biometric Identification System | Also a former INS system, it contains fingerprints of people caught violating immigration laws. It also stores the biometric information collected by US-VISIT. | Legacy INS data, new ICE data, and US-VISIT | ICE | IDENT data are being augmented by all nonimmigrant aliens in US-VISIT.<br><br>It is not clear how long data from legitimate visitors will be stored or when data will be destroyed.[e] |
| SEVIS | Student Exchange Visitor Information System | System used to register and track foreign students in the United States | Secondary schools, vocational schools, universities and colleges that enroll foreign students | ICE | SEVIS had been under development for several years but participation was made mandatory for any institution enrolling foreign students on January 30, 2003.[f]<br><br>System may be accessed from any Internet terminal or through secure data exchange. Each student in SEVIS is identified by a unique number associated with his or her I-20 form |

**Table A.1—Continued**

| Database | Definition | Description | Data Source | Data Owner | Notes |
|---|---|---|---|---|---|
| CLAIMS3 | Computer-Linked Application Information Management System | System holding biographic data on individuals who request federal benefits, changes in immigration status, and who have submitted fee payments to USCIS | USCIS benefits, Freedom of Information Act, claims, and other requests | USCIS | The CLAIMS4 system also exists.[g] This system was also previously managed by INS. |
| CCD | Consular Consolidated Database | "Database aggregating data from all U.S. consular activities abroad including visa issuance, passport replacement, and births and deaths of American citizens"[h] | U.S. Department of State and overseas consulates | DOS | Fully operational in 1991,[h] the system has been augmented to include biometric visa data from foreign travelers. |
| | | Air and sea carrier manifest data | Passengers and travel agencies | Individual air and sea carriers | Each air carrier maintains its own reservation database to serve particular business needs. Communication with government agencies typically takes the form of the Passenger Name Record (PNR), which includes personal and flight information.[i] |

SOURCE: Hite (2004b).

[a] See U.S. Department of Homeland Security, "Fact Sheet: US-VISIT Program" (undated), for a description of the interactions among US-VISIT databases.
[b] Krouse and Perl (2001).
[c] BATF = Bureau of Alcohol, Tobacco, and Firearms.
[d] IBIS was originally developed by the Immigration and Naturalization Service and the U.S. Customs Service to provide lookout information to federal agencies involved in the inspection of goods and persons. As such, it includes data regarding immigration violators and persons involved in smuggling (see Krouse and Perl, 2001).
[e] U.S. Department of Homeland Security, "US-VISIT Privacy Policy" (undated). The US-VISIT privacy policy states that "Personal information collected by US-VISIT will be retained and destroyed in accordance with applicable legal and regulatory requirements," but it does not specify what these requirements are; it is assumed that US-VISIT will abide by the privacy policy posted on its Web site.
[f] Hamilton (2003).
[g] See U.S. Citizenship and Immigration Services (2005d) for a description of CLAIMS.
[h] Fulton (2002).
[i] U.S. Bureau of Customs and Border Protection (2004).

# US-VISIT Ports of Entry

**Table B.1**
**US-VISIT Air Ports of Entry**

| Location | Airport |
| --- | --- |
| Agana, Guam | Agana International Airport |
| Aguadilla, Puerto Rico | Rafael Hernandez Airport |
| Albuquerque, New Mexico | Albuquerque International Airport |
| Anchorage, Alaska | Anchorage International Airport |
| Aruba | Pre-Flight Inspection |
| Atlanta, Georgia | William B. Hartsfield International Airport |
| Austin, Texas | Austin Bergstrom International Airport |
| Baltimore, Maryland | Baltimore/Washington International Airport |
| Bangor, Maine | Bangor International Airport |
| Bellingham, Washington | Bellingham International Airport |
| Boston, Massachusetts | General Edward Lawrence Logan International Airport |
| Brownsville, Texas | Brownsville/South Padre Island Airport |
| Buffalo, New York | Greater Buffalo International Airport |
| Calgary, Canada | Pre-Flight Inspection |
| Chantilly, Virginia | Washington Dulles International Airport |
| Charleston, South Carolina | Charleston International Airport |
| Charlotte, North Carolina | Charlotte/Douglas International Airport |
| Chicago, Illinois | Chicago Midway Airport |
| Chicago, Illinois | Chicago O'Hare International Airport |
| Cincinnati, Ohio | Cincinnati/Northern Kentucky International Airport |
| Cleveland, Ohio | Cleveland Hopkins International Airport |
| Columbus, Ohio | Rickenbacker International Airport |

**Table B.1—Continued**

| Location | Airport |
|---|---|
| Columbus, Ohio | Port Columbus International Airport |
| Dallas/Fort Worth, Texas | Dallas/Fort Worth International Airport |
| Del Rio, Texas | Del Rio International Airport |
| Denver, Colorado | Denver International Airport |
| Detroit, Michigan | Detroit Metropolitan Wayne County Airport |
| Dover/Cheswold, Delaware | Delaware Airpark |
| Dublin, Ireland | Pre-Flight Inspection |
| Edmonton, Canada | Pre-Flight Inspection |
| El Paso, Texas | El Paso International Airport |
| Erie, Pennsylvania | Erie International Airport |
| Fairbanks, Alaska | Fairbanks International Airport |
| Fajardo, Puerto Rico | Diego Jimenez Torres Airport |
| Fort Lauderdale, Florida | Fort Lauderdale Executive Airport |
| Fort Lauderdale, Florida | Fort Lauderdale/Hollywood International Airport |
| Fort Myers, Florida | Fort Myers International Airport |
| Freeport, Bahamas | Pre-Flight Inspection |
| Greenville, South Carolina | Donaldson Center Airport |
| Hamilton, Bermuda | Pre-Flight Inspection |
| Hartford/Springfield, Connecticut | Bradley International Airport |
| Honolulu, Hawaii | Honolulu International Airport |
| Houston, Texas | Houston International Airport |
| Indianapolis, Indiana | Indianapolis International Airport |
| International Falls, Minnesota | Falls International Airport |
| Isla Grande, Puerto Rico | Isla Grande Airport |
| Jacksonville, Florida | Jacksonville International Airport |
| Juneau, Alaska | Juneau International Airport |
| Kansas City, Kansas | Kansas City International Airport |
| Kenmore, Washington | Kenmore Air Harbor |
| Key West, Florida | Key West International Airport |
| King County, Washington | King County International Airport |
| Kona, Hawaii | Kona International Airport |

**Table B.1—Continued**

| Location | Airport |
|---|---|
| Laredo, Texas | Laredo International Airport and Laredo Private Airport |
| Las Vegas, Nevada | McCarren International Airport |
| Los Angeles, California | Los Angeles International Airport |
| Manchester, New Hampshire | Manchester Airport |
| Mayaguez, Puerto Rico | Eugenio Maria de Hostos Airport |
| McAllen, Texas | McAllen Miller International Airport |
| Memphis, Tennessee | Memphis International Airport |
| Miami, Florida | Kendall/Tamiami Executive Airport |
| Miami, Florida | Miami International Airport |
| Milwaukee, Wisconsin | General Mitchell International Airport |
| Minneapolis/St. Paul, Minnesota | Minneapolis–St. Paul International Airport |
| Montreal, Canada | Pre-Flight Inspection |
| Nashville, Tennessee | Nashville International Airport |
| Nassau, Bahamas | Pre-Flight Inspection |
| New Orleans, Louisiana | New Orleans International Airport |
| New York, New York | John F. Kennedy International Airport |
| Newark, New Jersey | Newark International Airport |
| Norfolk, Virginia | Norfolk International Airport and Norfolk Naval Air Station |
| Oakland, California | Metropolitan Oakland International Airport |
| Ontario, California | Ontario International Airport |
| Opa Locka/Miami, Florida | Opa Locka Airport |
| Orlando, Florida | Orlando International Airport |
| Orlando/Sanford, Florida | Orlando/Sanford Airport |
| Ottawa, Canada | Pre-Flight Inspection |
| Philadelphia, Pennsylvania | Philadelphia International Airport |
| Phoenix, Arizona | Phoenix Sky Harbor International Airport |
| Pittsburgh, Pennsylvania | Pittsburgh International Airport |
| Ponce, Puerto Rico | Mercedita Airport |
| Portland, Maine | Portland International Jetport Airport |
| Portland, Oregon | Portland International Airport |
| Portsmouth, New Hampshire | Pease International Tradeport Airport |

**Table B.1—Continued**

| Location | Airport |
|---|---|
| Providence, Rhode Island | Theodore Francis Green State Airport |
| Raleigh/Durham, North Carolina | Raleigh/Durham International Airport |
| Reno, Arizona | Reno/Tahoe International Airport |
| Richmond, Virginia | Richmond International Airport |
| Sacramento, California | Sacramento International Airport |
| Salt Lake City, Utah | Salt Lake City International Airport |
| San Antonio, Texas | San Antonio International Airport |
| San Diego, California | San Diego International Airport |
| San Francisco, California | San Francisco International Airport |
| San Jose, California | San Jose International Airport |
| San Juan, Puerto Rico | Luis Muñoz Marin International Airport |
| Sandusky, Ohio | Griffing Sandusky Airport |
| Sarasota/Bradenton, Florida | Sarasota-Bradenton International Airport |
| Seattle, Washington | Seattle/Tacoma International Airport |
| Shannon, Ireland | Pre-Flight Inspection |
| Spokane, Washington | Spokane International Airport |
| St. Croix, Virgin Island | Alexander Hamilton International Airport |
| St. Louis, Missouri | St. Louis International Airport |
| St. Lucie, Florida | St. Lucie County International Airport |
| St. Petersburg, Florida | Albert Whitted Airport |
| St. Thomas, Virgin Island | Cyril E. King International Airport |
| Tampa, Florida | Tampa International Airport |
| Teterboro, New Jersey | Teterboro Airport |
| Toronto, Canada | Pre-Flight Inspection |
| Tucson, Arizona | Tucson International Airport |
| Vancouver, Canada | Pre-Flight Inspection |
| Victoria, Canada | Pre-Flight Inspection |
| West Palm Beach, Florida | Palm Beach International Airport |
| Wilmington, North Carolina | Wilmington International Airport |
| Winnipeg, Canada | Pre-Flight Inspection |
| Yuma, Arizona | Yuma International Airport |

SOURCE: U.S. Department of Homeland Security (2004a).

**Table B.2**
**US-VISIT Sea Ports of Entry**

| Location |
| --- |
| Galveston, Texas |
| Jacksonville, Florida |
| Long Beach, California |
| Miami, Florida |
| Port Canaveral, Florida |
| San Juan, Puerto Rico |
| San Pedro, California |
| Seattle, Washington (Cruise Terminal) |
| Seattle, Washington |
| Tampa, Florida (Terminal 3) |
| Tampa, Florida (Terminal 7) |
| Vancouver, Canada (Ballantyne Pier) |
| Vancouver, Canada (Canada Place) |
| Victoria, Canada (Pre Inspection) |
| West Palm Beach, Florida |

SOURCE: U.S. Department of Homeland Security (2004a).

**Table B.3**
**The 50 Busiest Land Ports of Entry in Fiscal Year 2002**

| Location |
| --- |
| San Ysidro, San Diego, California |
| Laredo-Lincoln, Juarez, Texas |
| Calexico, California |
| Hidalgo, Texas |
| Paso Del Norte, El Paso, Texas |
| Otay Mesa, San Diego, California |
| Laredo Air Field, Convent Street, Texas |
| Queenston Bridge, Lewiston, New York |
| Rainbow Bridge, Niagara Falls, New York |
| San Luis, Arizona |

**Table B.3—Continued**

| Land Port of Entry |
| --- |
| Nogales East, Arizona |
| Bridge of the Americas (BOTA), El Paso, Texas |
| Ysleta, El Paso, Texas |
| Douglas, Arizona |
| Gateway, Brownsville, Texas |
| Calexico East, Imperial Valley |
| Detroit Ambassador Bridge, California |
| Peace Bridge, Buffalo, New York |
| Detroit Tunnel, Michigan |
| Pharr, Texas |
| Del Rio, Texas |
| B&M Bridge, Brownsville, Texas |
| Eagle Pass II, Texas |
| Blue Water Bridge, Port Huron, Michigan |
| Los Tomates, Brownsville, Texas |
| Progreso, Texas |
| Eagle Pass, Texas |
| Sault Ste. Marie, Michigan |
| Mariposa, Nogales West, Arizona |
| Andrade, California |
| Roma, Texas |
| Pacific Highway, Blaine, Washington |
| Peace Arch, Blaine, Washington |
| Champlain, New York |
| Los Indios, Texas |
| Tecate, California |
| Rio Grande City, Texas |
| Massena, New York |
| Calais, Ferry Point, Maine |
| Alexandria Bay, Thousand Island, New York |
| International Falls, Minnesota |

**Table B.3—Continued**

| Land Port of Entry |
| --- |
| Stanton Street Bridge, Texas |
| Presidio, Texas |
| Sumas, Washington |
| Laredo, Columbia, Texas |
| Lukeville, Arizona |
| Derby Line, Vermont |
| Point Roberts, Washington |
| Fabens, Texas |
| World Trade Bridge, Laredo IV, Texas |

SOURCE: U.S. Department of Homeland Security (2004a).

# US-VISIT Ports of Exit

**Table C.1**
**US-VISIT Air Ports of Exit**

| Location | Airport | Date of Implementation |
|---|---|---|
| Baltimore, Maryland | Baltimore-Washington International | January 2004 |
| Chicago, Illinois | Chicago O'Hare International Airport | August 2004 |
| Atlanta, Georgia | William B. Hartsfield International Airport | September 2004 |
| Dallas/Fort Worth, Texas | Dallas/Fort Worth International Airport | September 2004 |
| Denver, Colorado | Denver International Airport | September 2004 |
| Detroit, Michigan | Detroit Metropolitan Wayne County Airport | September 2004 |
| Newark, New Jersey | Newark International Airport | September 2004 |
| Philadelphia, Pennsylvania | Philadelphia International Airport | September 2004 |
| Phoenix, Arizona | Phoenix Sky Harbor International Airport | September 2004 |
| San Francisco, California | San Francisco International Airport | September 2004 |
| San Juan, Puerto Rico | Luis Muñoz Marin International Airport | September 2004 |
| Seattle, Washington | Seattle/Tacoma International Airport | September 2004 |

SOURCE: U.S. Department of Homeland Security (2004b).

**Table C.2**
**US-VISIT Sea Ports of Exit**

| Location | Seaport | Date of Implementation |
|---|---|---|
| Miami, Florida | Port of Miami (cruise line terminals) | January 2004 |
| Los Angeles, California | San Pedro and Long Beach Seaport | September 2004 |

SOURCE: U.S. Department of Homeland Security (2004b).

# Privacy and Fair Information Practices

Since the early days of networked computer technology, automated personal data systems have been used to collect, manage, and store large quantities of information identifying and describing human subjects and their behavior. As technology enables personal information to be generated, captured, stored, and transmitted, a variety of issues must be considered.

- *Collection limitations.* Individuals or organizations usually want the ability to control what data are collected, when they are collected, and who is allowed to see them. Data are often provided so long as data-use policies are made clear and followed. These policies are usually either opt-in (use these data unless told not to) or opt-out (do not use these data unless given permission). US-VISIT proposes to access data initially collected for another purpose, such as data contained in SEVIS on foreign students.
- *Data usage.* Once the data are collected, it is not always clear how the data are used. Many times, the data form part of a historical record that is useful in later interactions, such as when visa histories are collected and analyzed.
- *Right of access and correction.* Capture of personal information can be either transparent (as when a transaction is logged) or opaque (as when a person fills out a form). However, once the data are in the hands of the recipient, the provider often has little say in what is recorded. Indeed, the information may later be sold or resold, or aggregated/commingled without the provider's knowledge or permission. The record may in fact be incorrect or incomplete, and in many cases the provider would like the right to look at and correct it. However, correction is complicated, since it is often unclear where the error originated and how it can be fixed. Such access is provided for credit information; an individual can request copies of his or her credit record yearly and update information as necessary. But in other domains, such as visa histories, access, if allowed, can be more difficult or more limited.[1]

---

[1] Section 222(f) of the Immigration and Nationality Act (8 U.S.C. 1202[f]) provides that records pertaining to the issuance or refusal of visas are confidential. It also specifies exceptions to the confidentiality rule: "(1) in the discretion of the Secretary of State certified copies of such records may be made available to a court which certifies that the information contained in such records is needed by the court in the interest of the ends of justice in a case pending before the court. (2) the Secretary of State, in the Secretary's discretion and on the basis of reciprocity, may provide to a foreign government information in the Department of State's computerized visa lookout database and, when necessary and appropriate, other records covered by this section related to information in the database (A) with regard to individual

- *Disclosure and openness.* Identity theft is the fastest-growing crime in the United States (Gordan, 2003). The Federal Trade Commission received 86,000 complaints about identity theft in 2002, comprising 43 percent of the total complaints it recorded—a 500 percent increase over a three-year period. Thus, although disclosure is desirable for identification and correction, it may not be desirable if the information can be used inappropriately.

- *Retention and disposal.* Some data items have limited lifespans; a credit transaction to pay for an airline ticket may disappear from a record a fixed period of time after payment is made. But in other cases, data are retained long after they are useful. Similarly, data disposal can become a concern if the disposal techniques raise the risk of inadvertent disclosure.

- *Security.* Often, different types of data are restricted to different types of users. Airline reservation agents may need to review travel history information, but the ability to review associated payment information may be restricted to employees of the accounting department. Security controls can be provided to restrict viewing or modification as appropriate.

- *Aggregation.* In some cases, individual data records can be protected from disclosure by using aggregation. However, there are ways to infer information about individuals from aggregations, so care must be taken to keep from disclosing individual content. Moreover, aggregated information is open to a wider audience and useful for a variety of purposes. For example, it may be unnecessary to reveal that a particular person has AIDS, but aggregated data can suggest what percentage of the general population has contracted AIDS and in what parts of a country or community.

- *Accountability.* When privacy is breached, it must be clear who is responsible for the negative outcomes and for fixing the problem.

- *Anonymity and pseudonymity.* There are many situations where anonymity or pseudonymity is desirable. For example, whistle-blowers should be able to provide information about misdeeds without jeopardizing their own careers or reputations.

In any consideration of privacy, then, it is essential to consider these aspects and to ensure that in enhancing one aspect, a rule or regulation does not diminish another aspect. Moreover, a desirable balance must be struck among the aspects; the pivotal question is, "What is an appropriate balance?"

In 1972, the Advisory Committee on Automated Data Systems was created through the U.S. Department of Health, Education, and Welfare with the charge to "analyze harmful consequences that might result from automated personal data systems. The Advisory Committee's goal was to make recommendations about safeguards that might protect individ-

---

aliens, at any time on a case-by-case basis for the purpose of preventing, investigating, or punishing acts that would constitute a crime in the United States, including, but not limited to, terrorism or trafficking in controlled substances, persons, or illicit weapons; or (B) with regard to any or all aliens in the database, pursuant to such conditions as the Secretary of State shall establish in an agreement with the foreign government in which that government agrees to use such information and records for the purposes described in subparagraph (A) or to deny visas to persons who would be inadmissible to the United States."

uals against potentially harmful consequences and afford them redress for any harm" (Ware, 1973). Following from its discussions, the Advisory Committee recommended the creation of a Federal "Code of Fair Information Practices" that would apply to all personal data systems, establishing standards of fair recordkeeping while protecting the rights of the individual whose records are being kept (U.S. Department of Health, Education, and Welfare, 1972). Although the Code was contained within the committee's report, the essence of its principles formed the basis of several subsequent pieces of legislation and sets of guidelines both in the United States and abroad over the next three decades.

The Code of Fair Information Practices, as it was introduced in the Advisory Committee's 1973 report, is based on five principles considered by the Committee to be the minimum set of rights that should be available to the individual (U.S. Department of Health, Education, and Welfare, 1972; Ware, 1973):

1. *Notice and awareness:* There must be no personal-data recordkeeping systems whose very existence is secret.
2. *Access and participation:* There must be a way for an individual to find out what information exists in a record and how it is used.
3. *Choice and consent:* There must be a way for an individual to prevent information about him or her that was obtained for one purpose from being used or made available for other purposes without consent.
4. *Enforcement and redress:* There must be a way for an individual to correct or amend a record of identifiable information.
5. *Integrity and security:* Any organization creating, maintaining, using, or disseminating records of identifiable personal data must assure the reliability of the data for their intended use and must take precautions to prevent misuse of the data.

The committee recommended that the Code be enacted through legislation that would require adherence to specified safeguards meant to protect the rights of individuals listed above and would provide real consequences for any unfair information practice. It was concluded that this approach was the only way to protect the rights of individuals without creating additional bureaucracy and red tape in the form of a government regulatory body (Ware, 1973; U.S. Department of Health, Education, and Welfare, 1972).

Following the release of the committee's findings, Congress passed the Privacy Act of 1974.[2] Though vastly different in scope, the Act is based on the Code of Fair Information Practices outlined by the Advisory Committee the previous year. The legislation protects the privacy only of personal data maintained by government agencies and their contractors (that is, the law does not cover personal or commercial databases); it also requires federal agencies and their contractors to ensure that adequate safeguards are used to prevent the misuse of such information. No subsequent federal legislation is devoted solely to the purpose of controlling

---

[2]   5 U.S.C. § 552a.

the use of personal data and protecting individual privacy. In general, control over the treatment of personal data by the private sector (other than those companies that are government contractors) or by other countries was left up to the individual state or foreign governments.

Shortly after the Code of Fair Information Practices was developed, the Organization for Economic Cooperation and Development (OECD) addressed the issue of personal data protection. In 1980, the OECD listed eight guidelines defining the fair collection, use, and protection of personal data; the individual's right to access his or her own information; and the flow of such information across borders.[3] The guidelines can be summarized as follows:

- *Collection limitation:* There should be limits to the collection of personal data and any such data should be obtained by lawful and fair means and, where appropriate, with the knowledge or consent of the data subject.
- *Data quality:* Personal data should be relevant to the purposes for which they are to be used, and, to the extent necessary for those purposes, should be accurate, complete, and kept up-to-date.
- *Purpose specification:* The purposes for which personal data are collected should be specified not later than at the time of data collection and the subsequent use should be limited to the fulfillment of those purposes or such others as are not incompatible with those purposes and as are specified on each occasion of change of purpose.
- *Use limitation:* Personal data should not be disclosed, made available, or otherwise used for purposes other than those specified in accordance with the specified purpose, except with the consent of the data subject or by the authority of law.
- *Security safeguards:* Personal data should be protected by reasonable security safeguards against such risks as loss or unauthorized access, destruction, use, modification, or disclosure of data.
- *Openness:* There should be a general policy of openness about developments, practices, and policies with respect to personal data. Means should be readily available of establishing the existence and nature of personal data, and the main purposes of their use, as well as the identity and usual residence of the data controller.
- *Individual participation:* An individual should have the right to obtain from a data controller, or otherwise, confirmation of whether or not the data controller has data relating to him or her and to have access to such data. These data should be made available within a reasonable time; at a charge, if any, that is not excessive; in a reasonable manner; and in a form that is readily intelligible to him or her. If a request for data is denied, reasons should be given for the denial, and the requester should be able to challenge the denial. If the challenge is successful, the requester has a right to have the data erased, rectified, completed, or amended.

---

[3]   The guidelines and their history are available on the OECD Web site at http://www.oecd.org/document/18/0,2340,en_2649_34255_1815186_1_1_1_1,00.html (as of January 11, 2006). These guidelines were reprinted in a later OECD document: *OECD Guidelines on the Protection of Privacy and the Transborder Flows of Personal Data* (Organisation for Economic Co-operation and Development, 2001).

- *Accountability:* A data controller should be accountable for complying with measures that give effect to the principles stated above.

In addition, the Council recommended that OECD member countries consider these guidelines when making new legislation in the future, work to remove unjustified obstacles to the trans-border flows of personal data, cooperate with one another in implementing these guidelines, and agree as soon as possible on a set of specific procedures for consultation and cooperation when applying these guidelines. Like the Code of Fair Information Practices, the OECD guidelines were an attempt to encourage comprehensive privacy legislation that would apply to the general collection and use of personal data.

In 1995, the European Union defined a personal privacy policy applying to all member countries. The Directive on the Protection of Individuals with Regard to the Processing of Personal Data and on the Free Movement of Such Data (Directive 95//EC, 1995) can be summarized in the following principles:

- *Purpose specification:* Data collected must be adequate and relevant to the purpose for which they are collected.
- *Collection limitations:* Data may not be further processed in ways incompatible with the purposes for which they are collected.
- *Openness:* Recipients of data are entitled to know where the data come from and the conditions under which they were collected.
- *Access:* Individuals should have full access to data linked to their identifying information and the right to correct any inaccurate data. Individuals also have the right to "opt out" of further processing or transmission of personal data.
- *Individual participation:* Processing of sensitive data containing information about individuals' race, ethnicity, religion, union memberships, political opinions, or sexual preferences cannot be processed without permission. In some cases, it cannot be processed even with the individual's permission.
- *Accountability:* Each country must have at least one public authority responsible for monitoring and enforcing the directive.

The directive applies not only to organizations within EU member countries but also to foreign organizations, such as airlines, that process information inside the EU. The directive contains guidelines to ensure that data are transferred outside the EU only when adequate protection is in place. Although the comprehensive policy simplifies privacy restrictions across the EU, these guidelines sometimes complicated and confused data transfer between the European Union and the United States. Without a similar policy to ensure "adequate" treatment of personal data passing from EU member states to the United States, data transfers were slowed or even blocked. A climate of uncertainty developed amid confusion over what the rules were, to whom they applied, and which parties would be held liable in specific circumstances. In an effort to alleviate some of this confusion, the U.S. Department of Commerce issued the Safe

Harbor Principles in July 2000.[4] By voluntarily adhering to these principles, U.S. companies and government agencies can attempt to demonstrate to EU countries with which they interact their commitment to personal privacy protection and to the prevention of future lawsuits over the misuse of personal data. The Safe Harbor Principles are based on the five principles of the Code of Fair Information Practice:

- *Notice.* An organization must inform individuals, clearly and conspicuously, of the purpose, use, and subsequent disclosure of any personal information collected that pertains to them.
- *Choice.* An organization must offer individuals the opportunity to choose (by initiating an opt-out action) whether or not their personal information is disclosed to a third party or used for a purpose other than that for which it was initially collected. In some situations involving sensitive information, the individual must give explicit authorization to the organization (by initiating an opt-in action) before these actions can take place.
- *Onward transfer.* Before disclosing personal information to a third party, the organization is responsible for making sure that the third party subscribes to the Safe Harbor Principles, is subject to the EU Directive, or has entered into a written agreement ensuring that it will provide at least the same level of privacy protection as the Principles demand.
- *Security.* An organization must take reasonable precautions against the loss; misuse; and unauthorized access, disclosure, alteration, or destruction of the personal information it possesses.
- *Data integrity.* Personal information must be relevant for the purposes for which it is to be used. An organization should take reasonable steps to ensure that data are reliable, accurate, complete, and current for their intended use.
- *Access.* Individuals must have access to personal information about them that an organization holds and be able to correct, amend, or delete that information where it is inaccurate, as long as doing so would not violate the rights of any other persons.
- *Enforcement.* Effective privacy protection must include mechanisms for assuring compliance with the Safe Harbor Privacy Principles, recourse for individuals to whom the data relate and who are affected by noncompliance with the Principles, and consequences for the noncompliant organization when the Principles are not followed (U.S. Department of Commerce, 2000).

---

[4]   Available at U.S. Department of Commerce (2000).

# References

Anderson, Robert H., Tora K. Bikson, Rosalind Lewis, Joy S. Moini, and Susan Straus, *Effective Use of Information Technology: Lessons About State Governance Structures and Processes*, Santa Monica, Calif.: RAND Corporation, MR-1704, 2003. Online at http://www.rand.org/pubs/monograph_ reports/MR1704/ (as of January 6, 2006).

Bowers, Faye, "U.S.-Mexican Border as a Terror Risk," *Christian Science Monitor*, March 22, 2005, p. 1.

Brown, Derek, "EEC Pledges Terrorist Fight, European Ministers Agree to Better Communication in Bid to Halt International Terrorism," *The Guardian (London)*, September 22, 1986.

Bush, George W., Homeland Security Presidential Directive 2, *National Security Presidential Directives*, Federation of American Scientists, Intelligence Resource Program, October 29, 2001. Online at http://www.fas.org/irp/offdocs/nspd/hspd-2.htm (as of January 6, 2006).

———, Homeland Security Presidential Directive 6, *National Security Presidential Directives*, Federation of American Scientists, Intelligence Resource Program, September 16, 2003. Online at http://www.fas.org/irp/offdocs/nspd/hspd-6.html (as of January 6, 2006).

———, Homeland Security Presidential Directive 11, *National Security Presidential Directives*, Federation of American Scientists, Intelligence Resource Program, August 27, 2004. Online at http://www.fas.org/irp/offdocs/nspd/hspd-6.html (as of January 6, 2006).

Directive 95//EC of the European Parliament and of the Council on the Protection of Individuals with Regard to the Processing of Personal Data and on the Free Movement of Such Data, Brussels, Belgium: European Economic Community, 1995.

Echikson, William, "Parisians Adapt to Anti-Terror Vigilance," *Christian Science Monitor*, October 7, 1986, p. 9.

"France Hit by Visa Control Backlash," *The Times (London)*, September 22, 1986.

Fulton, Barry, *Leveraging Technology in the Service of Diplomacy: Innovation in the Department of State*, Washington, D.C.: George Washington University, School of Media and Public Affairs, 2002.

Gordan, Marne, "Catch Me If You Can; How to Prevent Identity Theft," *Computerworld*, February 26, 2003. Online at http://www.computerworld.com/securitytopics/security/story/0,10801,78829,00. html (as of January 11, 2006).

Graham, George, "French Visa Rules Stamp on Tourism, *Financial Times*, August 11, 1987, p. 2.

Hamilton, Kendra, "Spending Time on SEVIS," *Black Issues in Higher Education*, September 11, 2003.

Hess, Ronnie, "Going to Paris? Don't Forget Toothbrush, Camera, and a Visa," *Christian Science Monitor*, May 14, 1987, p. 9.

Hite, Randolph C., *Risks Facing Key Border and Transportation Security Program Need to Be Addressed*, GAO-04-569T, Washington, D.C.: Government Accountability Office, March 18, 2004a.

———, *First Phase of Visitor and Immigration Status Program Operating, but Improvements Needed*, GAO-04-586, Washington, D.C.: General Accounting Office, May 11, 2004b.

Hollifield, James, "Ideas, Institutions and Civil Society: On the Limits of Immigration Control in France," paper delivered at Workshop on Immigration Control in Europe, Center for International and European Law on Immigration and Asylum, Southern Methodist University, Dallas, Tex., 1997.

Jacobs, Janice, Deputy Assistant Secretary of State for Visa Services, "Creating Secure Borders and Open Doors: Review of Department of Homeland Security–State Department Collaboration on Visa Policy," congressional testimony to the House Government Reform Committee, September 9, 2004. Online at http://travel.state.gov/law/legal/testimony/testimony_2137.html (as of January 6, 2006).

Krouse, William J., and Raphael F. Perl, *Terrorism: Automated Lookout Systems and Border Security Options and Issues*, Washington, D.C.: Library of Congress, Congressional Research Service, 2001.

Latour and Lleras, P.A., "Update on Efforts to Repeal Section 110 of IIRIRA," *U.S. Visa News*, April 20, 2000. Online at http://www.usvisanews.com/articles/memo949.shtml (as of January 6, 2006).

Lebon, André, *1986–1987: Le Point sur L'immigration et la Présence Éntragère en France*, Paris: La Documentation française, 1988.

———, *Immigrés et Éntragers en France: Tendances 1988/MI-1989*, Paris: La Documentation française, 1989.

———, *Regard sur L'immigration et la Présence Éntragère en France: 1989/1990*, Paris: La Documentation française, 1990.

Masuda, Funai, Eifert and Mitchell, Ltd., "DHS Suspends Certain Provisions of the Special Registration Program but Does Not Entirely Eliminate the Program," *Legal Updates, Immigration*, Masuda, Funai, Eifert and Mitchell, Attorneys at Law, December 1, 2003. Online at http://www.masudafunai.com/eng/legalupdates/index.asp?EXPAND=2003&F_YEAR=2003&aid=7&F_KEYWORD=&a=false&cid=2#251 (as of January 6, 2006).

*Memorandum of Understanding Between the Secretaries of State and Homeland Security Concerning Implementation of Section 428 of the Homeland Security Act of 2002*, Washington, D.C.: U.S. Department of State and U.S. Department of Homeland Security, 2003.

Miller, Judith, "Prime Minister of France Pledges 'Crushing' Response to Bombings," *The New York Times*, September 18, 1986, p. 1.

O'Connor, Patrick D. T., *Practical Reliability Engineering*, fourth ed., West Sussex, U.K.: John Wiley and Sons, Inc., 2002.

O'Harrow, Robert, and Jr. Scott Higham, "2-Fingerprint Border ID System Called Inadequate," *The Washington Post*, October 19, 2004, p. A08. Online at http://www.washingtonpost.com/wp-dyn/articles/A43276-2004Oct18.html (as of January 24, 2006).

Organisation for Economic Co-operation and Development, *OECD Guildelines on the Protection of Privacy and the Transborder Flows of Personal Data*, Paris, 2001.

Passel, Jeffery S., "Mexican Immigration: A U.S. Perspective," presentation at the Institute for Legal Research, National Autonomous University of Mexico, Mexico City, November 25, 2003. Cited in *Managing Mexican Migration to the United States: Recommendations for Policy Makers*, Washington, D.C.: Center for Strategic and International Studies and Instituto Tecnológico Autónomo de México, April 2004. Online at http://www.csis.org/media/csis/pubs/binational_council_migration.pdf (as of January 6, 2006).

The Perryman Group, *Stalling the Engine of Growth in a Global Economy: The Impact of Implementation of the US-VISIT Program at US-Mexico Border Crossings on Business Activity in the US, Texas, and the Border Region*, Waco, Tex., 2004.

Public Law 104-208, Illegal Immigration Reform and Immigrant Responsibility Act (IIRIRA), September 30, 1996.

———— 106-215, Data Management Improvement Act (DMIA), June 15, 2000.

———— 106-396, Visa Waiver Permanent Program Act (VWPPA), October 30, 2000.

———— 107-56, Uniting and Strengthening America by Providing Appropriate Tools Required to Intercept and Obstruct Terrorism (USA PATRIOT) Act, October 24, 2001.

"Report: Canada's Border Not Secure," CBS News, December 15, 2004. Online at http://www.cbsnews.com/stories/2004/12/15/world/main661313.shtml (as of January 6, 2006).

Rosenberg, Paul, The US-VISIT Program: A Seminar, Arlington, Va., August 3, 2004.

Ryan, Sid, "Most Important Link," *The Toronto Sun*, October 7, 2005. Online at http://torontosun.canoe.ca/News/Columnists/Ryan_Sid/2005/10/07/1251730.html (as of January 6, 2006).

Seghetti, Lisa M., *U.S. Visitor and Immigrant Status Indicator Technology Program (US-VISIT)*, RL32234, Washington, D.C.: Library of Congress, Congressional Research Service, 2004.

"The Terrorists of France: Editorial," *The Journal of Commerce*, October 28, 1986, p. 15A.

United Nations, *Statistical Yearbook*, fortieth issue, New York: United Nations, Department of Economic and Social Affairs, Statistics Division, 1993.

United Nations Statistics Division, Common Database, "Tourist Arrivals by Region of Origin," code series 28310, undated. Online at http://unstats.un.org/unsd/cdb/cdb_advanced_data_extract_yr.asp?HSrID=28310&HCrID=250 (as of January 11, 2006).

U.S. Code, Title 5, Government Organization and Employees, Section 552a, Records Maintained on Individuals, January 3, 2005.

————, Title 8, Aliens and Nationality, Section 1104, Powers and Duties of the Secretary of State, January 3, 2005.

————, Title 8, Aliens and Nationality, Section 1202, Application for Visas, January 3, 2005.

U.S. Bureau of Customs and Border Protection, *Undertakings of the Department of Homeland Security Bureau of Customs and Border Protection*, U.S. Department of Homeland Security, 2004. Online at http://www.dhs.gov/interweb/assetlibrary/CBP-DHS_PNRUndertakings5-25-04.pdf (as of September 2, 2004).

U.S. Citizenship and Immigration Services, *Executive Summary: Estimates of the Unauthorized Immigrant Population Residing in the United States: 1990 to 2000*, January 31, 2003a. Online at http://www.uscis.gov/graphics/shared/statistics/publications/2000ExecSumm.pdf (as of January 6, 2006).

————, "H-1B Frequently Asked Questions," October 30, 2003b. Online at http://uscis.gov/graphics/howdoi/h1b.htm (as of January 6, 2006).

————, "Immigration Classifications and Visa Categories," September 7, 2005a. Online at http://uscis.gov/graphics/services/visa_info.htm (as of January 6, 2006).

————, "Immigration Classifications and Visa Categories: Nonimmigrant Visas," September 7, 2005b. Online at http://uscis.gov/graphics/services/visas.htm (as of January 6, 2006).

————, "Students," September 23, 2005c. Online at http://uscis.gov/graphics/services/tempbenefits/StudVisas.htm (as of January 6, 2005).

————, Computer Linked Application Information Management System (CLAIMS 3 and 4), JUSTICE/INS-013, September 26, 2005d. Online at http://uscis.gov/graphics/aboutus/foia/ereadrm/013.htm (as of January 6, 2006).

U.S. Department of Commerce, "Safe Harbor Privacy Principles," July 21, 2000. Online at http://www.ita.doc.gov/td/ecom/SHPRINCIPLESFINAL.htm (as of January 11, 2006).

U.S. Department of Health, Education, and Welfare, *Records, Computers and the Rights of Citizens: Report of the Secretary's Advisory Committee on Automated Personal Data Systems*, Washington, D.C., 1972.

U.S. Department of Homeland Security, "Fact Sheet: US-VISIT Program," undated. Online at http://www.dhs.gov/dhspublic/display?theme=43&content=736 (as of January 6, 2006).

————, "US-VISIT: How It Works," undated. Online at http://www.dhs.gov/dhspublic/interapp/editorial/editorial_0525.xml (as of January 6, 2006).

————, "US-VISIT Privacy Policy," undated. Online at http://www.dhs.gov/dhspublic/interapp/editorial/editorial_0693.xml (as of January 6, 2006).

————, "US-VISIT Privacy Principles," undated. Online at http://www.dhs.gov/dhspublic/interapp/editorial/editorial_0681.xml (as of January 6, 2006).

————, "Departments of State, Homeland Security Reach Agreement on Visa Oversight Rule to Better Secure America's Borders," September 29, 2003a. Online at http://www.dhs.gov/dhspublic/display?content=1775 (as of January 6. 2006).

————, *Suspending the 30-Day and Annual Interview Requirements from the Special Registration Process for Certain Nonimmigrants; Interim Rule*, 8 CFR Part 264, Washington, D.C., December 2, 2003b. Online at http://www.uscis.gov/graphics/lawsregs/fr120203.pdf (as of January 11, 2006).

————, *U.S. Visit: Questions and Answers*, December 31, 2003c. Online at http://www.dhs.gov/interweb/assetlibrary/veryFINALRevised_FAQs12-31-2003.pdf (as of January 24, 2006).

————, "US-VISIT Ports of Entry," January 5, 2004a. Online at http://www.dhs.gov/interweb/assetlibrary/USVisit_PortsOfEntry.pdf (as of January 11, 2006).

————, "Department of Homeland Security to Begin Biometric Exit Pilot as Part of US-VISIT Program," press release, August 3, 2004b. Online at http://www.dhs.gov/dhspublic/display?content=3875 (as of January 25, 2006).

U.S. Department of Homeland Security, Office of the Inspector General, *Implementation of the United States Visitor and Immigrant Status Indicator Technology Program at Land Border Ports of Entry*, OIG-05-11, Washington, D.C.: U.S. Department of Homeland Security, 2005.

U.S. Department of State, Bureau of Consular Affairs, "New Requirements for Travelers," undated. Online at http://travel.state.gov/travel/cbpmc/cbpmc_2223.html (as of June 8, 2006).

———, "The U.S. Electronic Passport," undated. Online at http://www.travel.state.gov/passport/eppt/eppt_2498.html (as of January 24, 2006).

U.S. Embassy in Mexico, "U.S.-Mexico at a Glance," undated. Online at http://mexico.usembassy.gov/mexico/migration.html (as of January 6, 2006).

U.S. Immigration and Customs Enforcement, "Fact Sheet: I-901 SEVIS Feed for F, M, and J Nonimmigrant Students and Exchange Visitors," U.S. Department of Homeland Security, September 1, 2004. Online at http://www.ice.gov/graphics/sevis/factsheet/090104_fs.htm (as of April 22, 2005).

U.S. International Trade Administration, *International Safe Harbor Privacy Principles*, April 19, 1999. Online at http://ita.doc.gov/td/ecom/shprin.html (as of January 6, 2006).

Ware, Willis, *Records, Computers and the Rights of Citizens*, Santa Monica, Calif.: RAND Corporation, P-5077, 1973.

Wasem, Ruth Ellen, Jennifer Lake, Lisa Seghetti, James Monke, and Stephen Viña, *Border Security: Inspection Practices, Policies, and Issues*, RL32399, Washington, D.C.: Library of Congress, Congressional Research Service, 2004.